the films of
EDDIE MURPHY

By Edward Gross

Pioneer Books, Inc.   *Las Vegas, Nevada*

ALSO BY THE SAME AUTHOR
•TREK: THE LOST YEARS
•THE UNOFFICIAL TALE OF BEAUTY AND THE BEAST
•THE MAKING OF THE NEXT GENERATION
•THE 25TH ANNIVERSARY ODD COUPLE COMPANION
•SECRET FILE: THE MAKING OF A WISEGUY
•BRUCE LEE: FISTS OF FURY
•THE DARK SHADOWS TRIBUTE BOOK (CO-AUTHOR)
•THE SECRET OF MICHAEL J. FOX'S SUCCESS

Designed and Edited by Hal Schuster
with production assistance from James R. Martin

Library of Congress Cataloging-in-Publication Data
Edward Gross, 1960—
    The Films of Eddie Murphy

    1.   The Films of Eddie Murphy (entertainment)
 I. Title

Published by Pioneer Books, Inc., 5715 N. Balsam Rd., Las Vegas, NV, 89130.

First Printing, 1990

EDWARD GROSS has written

widely on the entertainment world. His articles covering the film and television industries appear in such diverse publications as *Premiere, Starlog, New York/Long Island Nightlife, Filmfax, Fangoria, Comics Scene, Total, The Island Ear, Teen Idols* and *Cinefantastique*. In addition, he co-wrote the story for an episode of ABC's *Supercarrier* and is the author of such nonfiction books as *Trek: The Lost Years, Secret File: The Making of a Wiseguy, The Making of the Next Generation, The 25th Anniversary Odd Couple Companion, Bruce Lee: Fists of Fury* and *The Secret of Michael J. Fox's Success*. He lives in New York, on Long Island, with his wife Eileen and their son, Teddy.

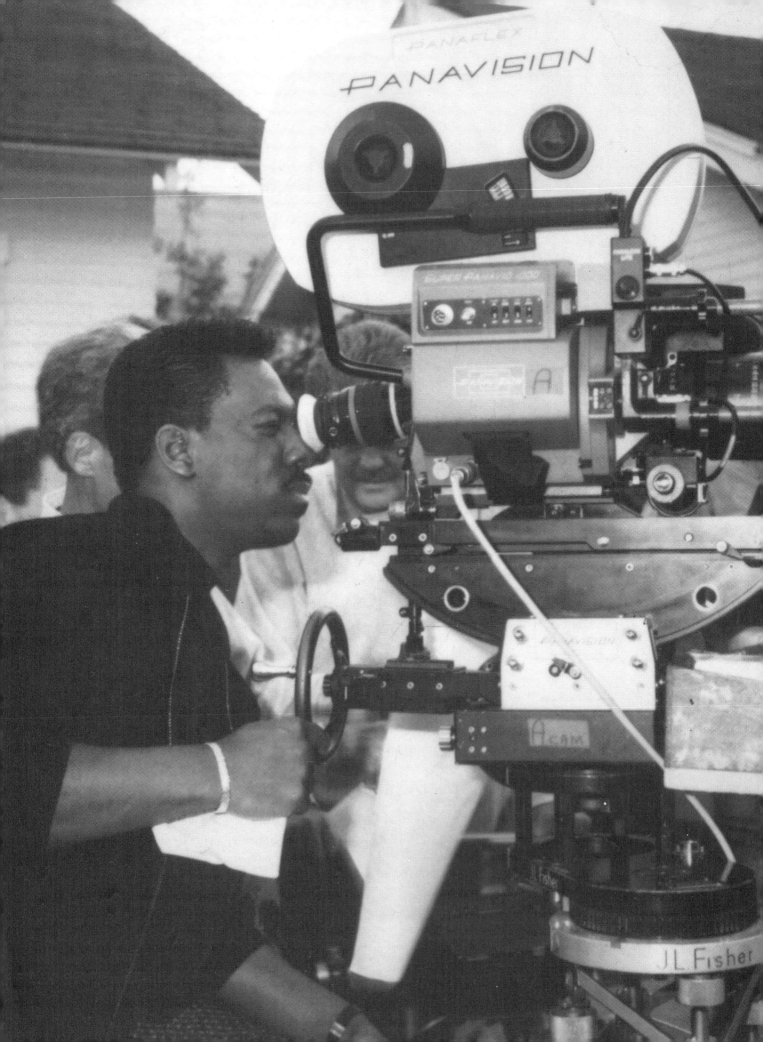

Contents Page....

An Introduction....

In the annals of Hollywood, there are only a handful of black actors who have successfully broken the color barrier to achieve worldwide success. Sidney Poitier, Bill Cosby, Richard Pryor and, of course, the late Sammy Davis, Jr. form a select group. The newest addition to the elite few, and one who has surpassed all of them in terms of box office popularity, is Eddie Murphy.

Murphy first captured national attention as a member of the 1980-81 ensemble group then on *Saturday Night Live*. That group of performers, who had the unenviable task of following in the footsteps of Chevy Chase, Dan Aykroyd, John Belushi, Gilda Radner and the rest of the Not Ready for Prime Time Players, was, for the most part, considered a dismal failure. The exceptions are Joe Piscopo, who has yet to parlay the fame he achieved into a successful film career, and Eddie Murphy, perhaps the most talented of the lot.

At the time, perhaps 70 minutes of *Saturday Night Live*'s 90 were fairly laughless; audience members groaned more than cheered. The laughs came whenever Eddie Murphy walked on stage—performing such incredible characters as Little Richard Simmons, Velvet Jones, Buckwheat and Gumby—and disappeared once he departed. Apparently Paramount Pictures sensed his impact. During the show's hiatus they signed him to co-star in Walter Hill's *48 Hrs.* with Nick Nolte. The film hit big, and the studio signed him to a multi-picture contract that made them both a lot of money.

Murphy delivered a series of films continually generating money at the box office, including *Trading Places, Beverly Hills Cop, Beverly Hills Cop II* and *Coming to America*. Between them lie such mediocre entries as *The Golden Child* and *Harlem Nights*. Only in comparison to the other films, could these be deemed financial failures. They grossed upwards of $100,000,000 each.

The Films of Eddie Murphy offers a comprehensive look at Murphy's motion pictures, combining an in-depth biography with a highly detailed filmography.

At the time of writing, *Another 48 Hrs.* is about to be released. Odds are strong it will continue the long line of successes that has greeted Eddie Murphy. He is a unique individual in Hollywood, constantly growing; attempting different venues of expression. He represents a true rags-to-riches story in the boldest tradition.

—**Edward Gross**

May, 1990

A Work in Progress

"Strangely enough, given my personal circumstances and the success of my films, I've got the worst deal in town. When I renegotiated my deal with Paramount a few years ago, it seemed great. But nobody planned that those pictures would be as successful as they were. So now I've got a shitty deal compared with what I could be making, one picture at a time for different studios. Take a studio like Columbia that's having bad luck with pictures. It would be more to my advantage to be with a smaller studio. At Disney or Warner's, I'd be the icing on the cake, but if I went to Columbia, I'd be the cake. And if nobody wants to give me a really lucrative deal, I'll just go independent and do my movies myself."

The speaker is Eddie Murphy, in *Playboy* magazine. In those pages, the actor, rather more colorfully, detailed his off-the-cuff thoughts concerning the imminent conclusion of his contract with Paramount Pictures. He has aligned himself with the studio since 1982.

The confidence etching his words is obvious. It's startling to note just how far he has come since his debut in *48 Hrs*. In the ensuing eight years, he has gone from a member of the *Saturday Night Live* ensemble to capturing the crown as king of the world's box office. His nine motion pictures grossed upwards of one billion dollars. Not too bad for a kid who grew up in Rockville, Long Island (in New York). And he only wanted to be funny.

"I was crazy," he explained. "I used to give shows in my basement and the edge of the carpet was the stage. I'd be Elvis and Al Green and Stevie Wonder and do all this for imaginary audiences.

"Even [in high school] I was *Eddie Murphy*. I was voted most popular. I was like a little celebrity. I had already been on local cable; I was a hot shot. In high school, I used to give assemblies. I did a show for the six grades over three days. My band played and afterward I did an hour of material about the school: impressions of teachers, students, hall monitors.... By the third day, people were sitting in the aisles. The truth is, I knew what I was put here to do.

"Until I was ten, I wanted to own a Mister Softee ice-cream truck. But after that, I knew I wanted to be in show business. Girls started screaming and I said, 'Shit, you can't make girls scream in a Mister Softee truck.'"

Murphy parlayed that desire of a fifteen year old into a stand-up routine performed at local Long Island and East Coast comedy clubs. He was an immediate hit.

"I'd do like five minutes of my own jokes," he said, "then go, 'Here's my tribute to Richard Pryor,' and do a half hour off his album."

Gradually more and more original material entered the act leading to his being signed at 18 as a *Saturday Night Live* regular. To viewers, and perhaps the producers, Murphy was the show's newest incarnation of Garrett Morris.

"It was just tokenism," Murphy told *Playboy*. "They just threw me in there to be the black guy on the show. They had no idea what was going to happen. I'd been on a year and they still didn't realize anything was happening."

Murphy honed his comic abilities, creating a wide variety of characters that left a lasting impression on his fans. Among those personas were Little Richard Simmons (a bizarre combination of rocker Little Richard and diet guru Richard Simmons), TV-Con Man Velvet Jones (whose products include the book *How to Be a Ho*), the white-people hating convict Tyrone Green, a larger than life Gumby (constantly saying, "I'm Gumby, damn it!") and Little Rascal, Buckwheat. With the possible exception of Joe Piscopo, Murphy was the only bright light in an otherwise lackluster cast that did nothing to make America forget the original Not Ready for Prime Time Players.

Recently, Murphy reflected warmly on the show, "When I left in 1984, I told every journalist that I hated the show. But, in retrospect, it was the most fun I ever had.

"I loved constantly being under the gun and having to write all the time. The criticism we got because we were 'those bastards who came along after Belushi' gave us a tougher skin. Everybody said, 'Hey, you the new guys on *Saturday Night Live?* Your show sucks!' And we were busting our arses up there, sixteen hours a day. When we finally overcame that, we did some good shows. That seems like a real long time ago. When I watch those old tapes, it weirds me out. I'm like this kid.

Sometimes I watch sketches and don't remember doing them.

"Now there's this onus on me—everything I do is under the magnifying glass. The world is watching. But back then it was new, and I didn't know anything about pressure. I was just having as much fun as I could. I was very creative back then, real hungry. You know the *Rocky* movies? 'You gotta get the eye of the tiger back, Rock!' I had it back then. I don't have the eye of the tiger anymore."

By the time Murphy left *SNL*, he was a critical and commercial success on the big screen surpassing other *SNL*ers with movie careers.

Bill Murray had hit it big with the one-two punch of *Meatballs* and *Stripes*; Chevy Chase had done well in *Foul Play*; John Belushi struck a chord with audiences in *National Lampoon's Animal House*—but Murphy was king. Murphy scored *big* with 1982's *48 Hrs.* and followed with *Trading Places*, beginning a winning streak that never quit.

48 Hrs. cast him as Reggie Hammond, a convict placed in the custody of Detective Jack Cates. Together they have 48 hours to track down Albert Ganz, wanted by the police for a spree of murders. Hammond has a personal reason for wanting him, too: half a million dollars their former gang stole from a drug sale. Hammond only has six months left on a three-year sentence, and doesn't want Ganz grabbing the money he has so patiently waited for.

The ingredients in *48 Hrs.* are perfect. It is one of the greatest buddy films ever made; magic sparks between Murphy and co-star Nick Nolte. Walter Hill provides wonderful direction and composer James Horner's adds one of his finest scores. The resulting mix of violence and humor pleased audiences and earned $100 million.

"Walter Hill was the first person to use that mix," Murphy pointed out. "*48 Hrs.* was the first movie where one minute somebody's being blown away, and the next [minute] you're laughing. I think *48 Hrs.* is the best movie I did, the best movie that Nick did and the best movie that Walter did. [It's] the most imitated movie of the Eighties. You can draw a line from it to *Commando* to *Lethal Weapon* to *Red Heat* to *Running Scared*. And none of them was as good as the original."

11

At the time of the film's release, director Walter Hill discussed those aspects of the film he thought worked particularly well. "The story is traditional urban thriller: two terrible guys are out there and have to be brought down," he said. "But even though I enjoy working in genres, the point is always to explode them or give them a transfusion. So I made a very conscious decision to go with the elements of personality of the two players, rather than be overly genuflective in the narrative. Thrusting a white policeman and a black convict together carries so much gravity that we didn't have to beat the white-black thing to death. If it works, it's because of the actors' personalities."

Why the choice of Murphy? Hill explains, "We never sent the script to any other actor. The advantage with Eddie is that you accept him as Reggie. It's not just a gifted comedian doing a star turn. He's got such a strong center, a strong feeling for who he is, yet at the same time he's only 21 years old. He's remarkable."

Murphy followed with *Trading Places*, a wonderfully old-fashioned comedy that cast him as con-man Billy Ray Valentine. The con-man is given the opportunity to trade his rags in for riches when he takes the place of Louis Winthorpe III (snootily, but endearingly, played by Dan Aykroyd). Winthorpe, a rich employee of the Duke and Duke Commodity Brokers company, is, in turn, reduced to poverty.

This manipulation of life arises courtesy of Randolph and Mortimer Duke (Ralph Bellamy and Don Ameche), two bored men of wealth engaged in a bet to determine whether a person is shaped by genes or environment. By film's end, Valentine and Winthorpe turn the tables on the Dukes via a manipulation of the stock market, elevating themselves to wealth and reducing the Dukes to poverty.

Eddie Murphy had already grown as an actor by the time he made this film. He retained the confidence displayed in *48 Hrs.*, but added more layers to his performance. When we meet Billy Ray Valentine, a street-wise con-man, Murphy delivers the proper "attitude." Later, when the con-man becomes a wealthy employee of Duke and Duke, the actor conveys a dramatic change in personality. He easily shifts into the lifestyle while maintaining the brains that kept him alive on the streets.

Murphy delivers a masterful performance when Valentine accidentally overhears

An early EDDIE MURPHY on SATURDAY NIGHT LIVE with Chevy Chase....

the Dukes refer to him as a "nigger". His reaction, when his eyes dart from side to side as though he's been unexpectedly slapped across the face, is a wonder to behold.

Murphy never takes a role too seriously, "I don't think I'll do any serious acting," he said some time ago. "*48 Hrs*. is about as heavy as I want to get. The big challenge for me is making somebody laugh. I put a hundred percent into my comedy. You just gotta have no doubts. I think that even the ugliest bitch in the world can say, 'I want to be a model'—and be one."

Next up was one of his most bizarre appearances, *Best Defense*. This one came with a peculiar billing, listing Murphy as a "strategic guest star". The film, a Dudley Moore vehicle, deals with the designer of a state-of-the-art tank (Moore) that has more than a couple of screws loose, and the army technician (Murphy) who is trying to teach American allies how to use it two years in the future. Apparently (and it really is a bit confusing), what Moore does in the past will effect what happens to Murphy in the future when the weapon must be used for defense purposes. Considering this was not a time-travel adventure, the premise doesn't make any sense.

Best Defense earned little at the box office. Murphy's noted, "It wasn't even my movie, but it always gets three or four lines in a story."

The actor goes out of his way to put down the film, infuriating film-makers Willard Huyck and Gloria Katz. They feel they had enough problems without Murphy's public comments. After all, no one forced him to take two million dollars for two weeks work.

Up to this point, Murphy had always been a co-star. *48 Hrs*. teamed him with Nick Nolte, *Trading Places* put him in with Dan Aykroyd and then, to a lesser degree, he played alongside Dudley Moore (hot after *10* and *Arthur*) in *Best Defense*. Murphy's next film put him on his own. And that catapulted Murphy to world domination at the box office.

Beverly Hills Cop had supposedly been in development at Paramount Pictures since 1974. The Daniel Petrie, Jr. screenplay was considered one of Hollywood's great unproduced scripts. According to *Esquire* magazine, producers Don Simpson and Jerry Bruckheimer wanted Murphy to portray protagonist Axel Foley, but a mix-up obliged Paramount to offer it to Sylvester Stallone.

Stallone tailored the script to himself, developing action set pieces while discarding humorous bits. In fact, the character's name transformed from Axel Foley to Axel Cobretti (Cobretti is the name Stallone later used in the 1986 film, *Cobra*).

Finally Paramount balked. The studio and Stallone agreed to disagree and parted company over creative differences. *Esquire* quoted a Paramount executive as saying, "'Most of the time, when they say 'creative differences', it means someone's ego got blown out of proportion. This was one time when creative differences really meant creative differences."

"I didn't read the original script," Murphy admitted, "but what happened was that Sly changed things around and when he rewrote the script, it became a different type of film. His *Beverly Hills Cop* was really *Cobra*, so he went off and made *Cobra* on his own."

In Murphy's capable hands, Foley is essentially a hybrid of Reggie Hammond and Billy Ray Valentine, with just the right touch of the stand-up comedian thrown in for good measure. He has the intelligence and wit of Hammond combined with the street savvy of Valentine.

Axel's best friend is killed after stealing bonds from his employer, and the Detroit cop tracks down Victor Maitland, the man who ordered the execution. The trail leads to Beverly Hills.

Arriving on the West Coast, he immediately butts heads with the police department. They handle things *very* differently than in Detroit—and most other places, for that matter. Ultimately he becomes friends with officers Taggert (John Ashton, late of TV's *Hardball*), Rosewood (Judge Reinhold), and Captain Bogomil (Ronny Cox, who portrayed "Dick" in *Robocop*). Together they take down the Maitland empire, becoming best friends in the process.

The real joy of *Beverly Hills Cop* is watching Murphy react to the denizens of Beverly Hills, as well as assume a variety of personas to con his way into various situations.

Murphy is a brilliant improvisationalist, and *Beverly Hills Cop* provides a wonderful showcase.

Commenting on Murphy, director Martin Brest told *Newsweek*, "He is a genius. I don't mean it like, 'Hey, you're a genius, baby.' I mean he's like nobody else around. It's spooky. He's so young. You wonder where he had time to pick up all this stuff. What he does is give the audience an opportunity to perceive things as perceptively as he does, and that's a thrill."

In the same publication, the actor replied, "I tell a good joke. But there's no such thing as a comic genius. Geniuses are people who do things with their brains—scientists, people with academic training. Not guys who play piano or make people laugh. I'd be the first to admit that I'm a very funny guy, and the last to admit I'm a genius."

Beverly Hills Cop grossed $300 million. The success gave Murphy carte blanche on his next project. Murphy initially began looking for something very different, and almost found it in *Star Trek IV: The Voyage Home*. That film, in which the crew of the starship Enterprise returns to the present to obtain a pair of humpback whales to save the future, was the most successful in the series. An early draft had been written for Murphy. In it, he would have portrayed the scientist who helps Captain Kirk, Mr. Spock and the rest of the crew achieve their goals. *Star Trek* fans, as is their wont, protested vehemently, drawing comparisons to the low-comedy of Richard Pryor co-starring in *Superman III*. They believed such a "team-up" could only spell disaster.

Murphy, for whatever reason, decided not to do the film. And so Paramount's two hottest box office properties never united.

"I've always wanted to do a *Star Trek*," he enthused. "I'm a Trekkie. I wanted to be in *Star Trek* and that's where they got the idea of coming back in time to Earth in 1987. The script was developed, but it didn't quite work out, so we dropped the idea. It was a choice between *Star Trek IV* and *The Golden Child*; and I chose *The Golden Child*, because I thought it would be better for my career. In retrospect, I might have been better off doing *Star Trek*."

The Golden Child, released in 1986, was definitely a change of pace. This time Murphy portrayed finder-of-lost-children Chandler Jarrell and entered the realm of fantasy and the supernatural.

In the film, servant of Satan Sardo Numspa (Charles Dance, who recently portrayed James Bond creator Ian Fleming in the BBC production *Goldeneye*) kidnaps a youth known as the Golden Child, and attempts to corrupt his pure soul, causing Earth to literally become Hell. Hope for mankind will be gone, unless Jarrell—the Chosen One—and the beautiful Mei Lei (Charlotte Lewis) are able to stop Numspa from obtaining a sacred dagger to kill the child. A series of bizarre adventures follows as Jarrell encounters one supernatural threat after another, always getting closer to his goal and outsmarting the best laid plans of the Devil.

Murphy delivers a nice turn as Jarrell, a character more concerned with helping children than making wisecracks and assuming other personas. Yet somehow Murphy seems out of place in this film. After the completion of shooting, comic moments similar to those Murphy created in previous films were added. They seem completely out of place.

The movie does provide an interesting contrast to Murphy's other films. Director Michael Ritchie t*Starlog* magazine, "The script is a contemporary supernatural sword and sorcery epic. It's something I might have had second thoughts about or just said, 'Why me?' to if I hadn't known that Eddie Murphy was committed to the project. Knowing that Eddie was involved gave the script a kind of perspective and humor in every scene. What I like about the movie is the contrast of the street-smart, wiseacre disbeliever caught up in a world of believers and magic in which he must ultimately believe. It's an exciting prospect.

"From the moment we did the screen tests for the girl, Eddie actually welcomed direction and I certainly was not sparing with it, or intimidated from giving it. Any good actor—and Eddie is a very good actor—welcomes that critical viewpoint. Eddie is probably the only comedy actor I've worked with—and I've worked with a lot: Chevy [Chase], Robin Williams, Gold [Hawn], Burt Reynolds—who *never* said to me, 'I'll be the judge of what's funny.' Usually at some point they pull rank on me and point out that they're the comedian and I'm not. That never happened with Eddie."

While the film would eventually gross $100 million, it was considered a major disappointment, following the phenomenal worldwide success of *Beverly Hills Cop*. Murphy remains philosophical, "*Golden Child* started out as a good picture. I don't think it's a bad movie. I think there are some bad things in it. I don't think it was done properly or looked quite right. I don't think *Golden Child* was what it could have been. I picked it because I wanted something where I wasn't shooting guns."

For his next project Murphy picked up his gun again, reprising the role of Axel Foley in the inevitable *Beverly Hills Cop II*. The film was originally going to be called *London Cop* until Murphy decided he didn't want to travel to the UK.

This time the trip west didn't work nearly as well. For all intents and purposes, it was a remake of its predecessor. The plot put Murphy on the trail of an alphabet killer, who seriously wounded Bogomil. Axel, upon hearing about this from Taggart and Rosewood, flies out to California to help.

Character relationships are taken a step beyond the first movie as we see the impact Axel has had on the lives of his friends, although the grittier look of the police station is a bit hard to swallow. Everything else conveys a disturbing sense of repetition.

It's interesting to compare Murphy's views of the film during its initial release and those he expressed more recently. "I knew I wanted to do a sequel to *Beverly Hills Cop* right after we finished the first one," he said in 1987. "I don't have any problems with doing sequels, and I think we'll continue with the films until the audience gets tired of them."

Yet in early 1990 he noted, "Do you know what's scary? *Beverly Hills Cop II* was probably the most successful mediocre picture in history. It made $250 million worldwide, and it was a half-arsed movie. *Cop II* was basically a rehash of *Cop I*, but it wasn't as spontaneous and funny. Paramount would love for me to turn *Beverly Hills Cop* into the *Police Academy* series. Americans are creatures of habit. That's why TV shows are so popular here. People like the idea of meeting somebody every week on a certain day, at a certain time, while sitting in the living room.

"There's no reason to do [*Beverly Hills Cop III*]. I don't need the money, and it's not gonna break any new ground. How often can you have Axel Foley talk fast and get into a place he doesn't belong? But [Paramount is] developing scripts for it. They're in preproduction. The only reason to do a *Cop III* is to beat the bank, and Paramount ain't gonna write me no check as big as I want to do something like that. In fact, if I do a *Cop III*, you can safely say, 'Oooh, he must have got a *lot* of money!' Two years ago I would have done it for a great big check; now I need a really great script *and* a good check. You know what I thought would have been the ideal *Beverly Hills Cop III*? *Die Hard*. Bruce Willis did a real good job. It's one of those movies I wish I was in."

Eddie Murphy's Raw was next, a concert film which quickly became the most successful in history, and one that has the distinction of almost being rated "X".

"Triple X," he's clarified with a laugh, "and that freaked me out, because I thought triple X was bestiality. We cut it and got an R, but it isn't as funny now. We had to take out a couple of jokes they thought were a bit too strong."

He followed with the feature *Coming to America*, a delightful comic excursion that took him to different plateaus as an actor. "Rather than go for the buck," Murphy detailed, "my impulse, after I did *Beverly Hills Cop II*, was to do something completely different. *Golden Child, Beverly Hills Cop, Beverly Hills Cop II* were the same character—Axel Foley—three movies in a row. After a while, people get tired of watching."

Bearing this in mind, it's not surprising that in 1987, Murphy had already begun considering a change in screen image. Nothing too dramatic, mind you, but certainly an approach that differed from what we'd seen before. In fact, at that time, during a press conference for *Beverly Hills Cop II*, he was forced to address a constant barrage of questions regarding a dramatic role and a romance in one of his future films.

"I know what I'm capable of doing and what I'm not capable of doing," he replied. "You won't see me doing a serious role. I find something that I like and conform it to myself. It's not that I can't do it, but I'm a little bit afraid of doing it. I think everybody's afraid of failure. Eventually there might be a time when I'll do a dramatic role, but does anybody really want to see a comedian in a serious movie? Do you look at someone who makes you laugh and say, 'I'd like to see him *not* make me

19

laugh?' As far as romance, eventually that will happen. I'm trying to stabilize my career before I start experimenting. I do dramatic action comedy, and there isn't a lot of time for romance. Otherwise, I'll shoot somebody, go home and say, 'Baby, I love you very much,' then go shoot somebody else. There's no sexuality in my Axel Foley movies. The one thing in *48 Hrs.* that I didn't like was the relationship between Nick Nolte's character and his girl. What does that have to do with the story? We're chasing these bad guys, and every now and then, he stops and goes [in Nolte's voice], 'Honey, I'm sorry I can't make dinner tonight, I'm chasing this killer.' Eventually I'd like to do a light comedy with romance."

He got his wish with *Coming to America.* He portrays the African prince, Akeem, who is distressed to learn that his parents (James Earl Jones and Madge Sinclair) have arranged his wedding to a woman he has never met. Exerting his independence, he and assistant/best friend Semmi (Arsenio Hall) head to the United States so that he can find a woman to fall in love with and marry. Their search takes them to Queens (what better place to find a future queen?), where they get jobs at McDowells, run by a proprietor blatantly ripping off McDonald's. Akeem eventually falls in love with the owner's daughter, Lisa (Shari Headley). What follows is a charming and delightful romance with Akeem winning Lisa over to himself, not his wealth and royal heritage. Naturally this leads to a conflict when Lisa learns the man she has fallen in love with is not who she thinks he is. The prince and his lady do eventually live happily ever after.

Coming to America is significant in that it gives Eddie Murphy the opportunity to do some real acting, elevating him far above his Reggie Hamond/Billy Ray Valentine/Axel Foley street-wise characterizations. Here he is touching, charming and, most important of all in a film that could have easily degenerated into an extended *SNL* skit, believable.

Critical reaction to the film was only lukewarm. The same people who put Murphy down for playing it safe in his choice of characters ignored his successful stretch into something different.

Arsenio Hall is terrific. The role launched him as an entertainment phenomenon in his own right. The rest of the cast delivered fine performances, especially those of the always wonderful James Earl Jones and newcomer Shari Headley. Director John

Landis, who hadn't had much box-office success since the tragic behind-the-scenes fatalities o*Twilight Zone: The Movie*, held his own, presenting a film quite different from his previous collaboration with Murphy, *Trading Places*.

There was considerable tension between Murphy and Landis during the production.

"He directed me in *Trading Places*," Murphy recently explained, "when I was just starting out as a kid, but he was still treating me like a kid five years later during *Coming to America*. And I *hired* him to direct the movie! I was gonna direct *Coming to America* myself, but I knew that Landis had just done three (problem) pictures in a row and that his career was hanging by a thread after the *Twilight Zone* trial. I figured the guy was nice to me when I did *Trading Places*, so I'd give him a shot. I'm a popular actor in this town, and (it) gave him some renewed credibility. I made Paramount hire him [and] he came in demanding lots of money. Paramount was saying, 'Hey, come on, Eddie,' but I made them pay his money. They bent over backward. But after he got the job, he brought along an *attitude*. He came in with this 'I'm a director' shit. Now he's got a hit picture on his resume, a movie that made over $200 million."

In terms of story, which Murphy purportedly penned, he has noted, "I think everybody who doesn't have somebody is looking for someone to call their own, even though they might say they *want* to be single. When I'm talking to my friends, I say the same thing about wanting to be single, but if I met the bomb tomorrow.

"I don't care who you are, what you have or what you did, there's always a woman out there who can bring you down to one knee. I can be brought to one knee, but the woman would have to have a helluva punch. I've been wobbled a couple of times already, but I haven't been to one knee. I'm not ready to commit to that whole straight up what's yours is mine and what's mine is yours, and having to look in the same person's face every day. You see, if someone is just your woman and not your wife, you can go off for a weekend and tell her to cool out for a few days. But you can't do that with your wife. You can't just say, 'Hey, baby, I need a week alone.' And right now I'm still at the point where a lot of times I need a week to be by myself.

"For me," he's added elsewhere, "*Coming to America* was a lesson in acting. Usually I'm the focus of the film, and they will put character actors in there to play parts around me. With the exception of a film like *48 Hrs.* , this is the first film in which I've learned something from other actors. Nobody can act like James Earl Jones, and no one is as classy as Madge Sinclair."

Rolling Stone asked Murphy if there could have been a film-maker such as Spike Lee without him.

"That's like saying there wouldn't be an Eddie Murphy if there wasn't a Richard Pryor," he responded. "Spike just does a different type of film than I do. Spike is more of a politician than I am. I'm an entertainer. If I can get a message across through my entertaining, fine. I think *Coming to America* is a political movie without shoving a message down anyone's throat. It's a black love story, in which black people are seen being black people, and it made $250 million. And that's a political statement without having to run a Malcolm X quote at the ending [as Lee did in *Do the Right Thing*]. Not that there's anything wrong with that. You can be overt or covert—you make the choice. I don't hold anything against the brother for being overt."

From a personal standpoint, *Harlem Nights* was undoubtedly his most challenging film. Murphy wrote, directed, produced and starred in the movie. Adding to the debuting director's apprehension was the fact that his co-stars included such veterans as Richard Pryor, Redd Foxx and Della Reese, all of whom were personal idols. While far from a masterpiece, *Harlem Nights* gives every indication that Murphy has a future ahead of him as a director.

The script, which many detractors compare unfavorably to *The Sting*, takes place in Harlem during the 1930's. Murphy is cast as Quick, adopted son to Richard Pryor's Sugar Ray, who, together, run the Club Sugar Ray. A thriving establishment, the club has raised the ire of the local mob kingpin who wants the business shut down. It's cutting into his profits. What follows is an elaborate sting operation in which Quick, Sugar Ray and their associates will leave New York with a considerable amount of the mobster's money.

Perhaps the film's greatest fault is that with the exception of the vehicles, this could very easily be a film taking place in 1990. The way people speak—particularly the foul language—makes it difficult to accept as a period piece. There are cliches aplenty, but enough strengths. Overall, Murphy delivers a credible job as scriptwriter.

Like Akeem in *Coming to America*, Quick is different from Murphy's typical on-screen persona. There's plenty of humor in the character, but also a startling ruthlessness.

"This guy's a hothead kid," Murphy has admitted. "Paramount was real weirded out by me playing such a hothead—somebody who shoots an old woman's pinkie toe off, who kills another woman who tried to kill him first. Paramount was unhappy, but I said, 'I'm an actor, man. I'm not gonna be Axel Foley every time I go up to the screen.' I'm happy about the movie and I'm proud of the way it turned out. It's not an action-packed kind of picture, and neither was *Coming to America*. But I wanted to get away from that because [the critics] pigeonhole you."

Murphy elaborated on his choice of this particular project in the pages of *Jet* magazine, "The thing that motivated me to make *Harlem Nights* is that for the last six years I've been making films and I've always wanted to work with Richard Pryor. I had bounced ideas off him lots of times but I couldn't come up with the ideal thing to do with Richard. I got the idea for the film from listening to his old albums. He used to do albums with crapshooters in the backroom and stuff like that. A lot of these characters were really potent characters and I thought that would be some good stuff to do a movie about. There hasn't been a film in recent years that has shown Harlem from a Black perspective, except for *Lady Sings the Blues*, which was a brilliant film [and co-starred Pryor]. [Film Producers] don't do Black period movies and I wanted to do a film like that. It was the perfect thing for Richard and me. Two guys own a gambling club and the mafia tries to take over the club. That sounds like a good movie. Then you take Redd Foxx, Della Reese, Jasmine Guy and Arsenio Hall and you've really got something special.

"Directing for the first time is intimidating, especially when you come to work the first day and have your idols looking to you for guidance. But they were so cool that after the first week I began to relax. Each day was better than the day before. It was sad when filming ended, but you can't feel too dejected after experiencing as much laughter as we did making *Harlem Nights*."

At summer 1990, Murphy's film career seems to have come full circle, as he reprises his role of Reggie Hammond in the sequel to his first film. *Another 48 Hrs.* reunites him with co-star Nick Nolte and director Walter Hill. Taking place five years after the original, this time it's detective Jack Cates (Nolte) who has 48 hours to apprehend a killer known as Iceman, who has framed him for murder. It seems the only person he can turn to is Hammond, who is released from prison and unhappily forced into working with Cates. Iceman happens to be the person that Reggie and his gang had stolen $500,000 prior to the events of the first film. Things are tense between the former partners, as Reggie has had the remaining six months of his original sentence extended to five years due to circumstances quite literally beyond his control. Cates, it seems, never came to visit him during that time. As far as Hammond is concerned, there's no love lost between them.

The magic between Murphy, Nolte and Hill are at work again. One can only hope that if there is a third entry, it will be produced with less than eight years between films.

Murphy noted shortly before the film's release, "Now we've got the original cast, director and producer. We made the one that everybody's trying to imitate, so we're trying to go one better. *48 Hrs.* is the best picture I've ever done as an actor, but the worst thing we can possibly do is try to recreate it. This time, I see more characterization, not bigger explosions."

Besides his astonishing film career, Murphy has carved an impressive niche for himself as a singer (*How Could It Be* and *So Happy*) and developed Eddie Murphy Productions. It's not only involved with each of his movies, but produces television pilots, including *What's Alan Watching?* and a proposed spinoff of *Coming to America*. Murphy sees no limits to his potential accomplishments, and has a very definite goal as noted in *Playboy* in 1983.

Seven years may have passed since he uttered his famous words, but it doesn't seem hard to believe they're as true today as they were then.

"I want to be more than big," he enthused. "I want to be *tremendous*. My goal is to be like—I wanna be like the Beatles, man. Like the Beatles were to music, that's what I want to be to comedy. That's my goal."

Despite his amazing success, EDDIE MURPHY still tackles every job as if his career, and life, depends on it....

The boys are back in town.
Nick Nolte is a cop. Eddie Murphy is a convict.

They couldn't have liked each other less... They couldn't have needed each other more.
And the last place they ever expected to be is on the same side.
Even for...

48 HRS.

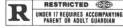

48 Hours....

Prior to the release of *48 Hrs.*, Eddie Murphy was an unknown quantity. Certainly he had attracted audiences to the latest incarnation of *Saturday Night Live*—ranking as one of the few standouts of his particular troupe—but few of his predecessors made the leap to big screen stardom.

Chevy Chase had hit it big with *Foul Play*, but then languished in a variety of box office failures until *National Lampoon's Vacation*. Dan Aykroyd scored with John Belushi in *The Blues Brothers*, a feature length version of an *SNL* skit, but failed in a number of films until *Ghostbusters*. More than a few people wondered what Murphy had to offer.

The answer came in *48 Hrs.*, one of the most auspicious motion picture debuts in recent years.

Director Walter Hill opens the film on a peaceful shot of horses grazing. The image creates the exact antithesis of what follows. Suddenly the horses flee in panic as tractors pass. Ultimately we see a group of prisoners at work on railroad tracks as armed guards patrol with shotguns. One prisoner, Albert Ganz, stares at a guard with unadulterated hatred in his eyes.

At that moment, a truck pulls up and a big Indian named Billy Bear gets out, asking for water because his engine is overheating. Ganz insults the Indian and the two get into a fist fight, landing in muddy water. Both surface armed with guns and blow away the nearby guards. A shootout with the other guards ensues as Ganz and Billy get in the truck and take off.

The scene changes. Jack Cates awakens and almost immediately gets into a fight with his girlfriend, Elaine. They're alternately friendly and hostile, and the audience learns this is will be a short-lived relationship.

The camera cuts to the streets of San Francisco, where Ganz is on a pay phone requesting hookers. Ganz uses the alias Polson and demands the women be sent to a particular hotel. As Ganz and Billy walk away, the camera shows someone lying dead on a park bench, a bullet hole in the center of his forehead.

Cates gets into his beat-up, roll-top Cadillac and drives off.

Elsewhere, Luther and his girlfriend Rosalie walk down a street, talking about an engagement ring. They're abruptly pulled into a car and held at gunpoint by Ganz and Billy Bear. Ganz wants "the" money and Luther insists he can't get it until Monday morning. Ganz considers this, adding that they're going to keep Rosalie to exchange for the money, so he'd better not screw up.

Picking up a police broadcast, Cates goes to a hotel and encounters Algran and Vanzant. Vanzant doesn't want him involved, but Algran says Jack can cover the lobby for them.

They enter and learn which room Polson occupies. They have heard a report that Ganz is using that man's stolen credit card.

In Ganz's room, he blankly watches a cartoon called *Space Kid*. While he watches, a nude prostitute talks to him, but he doesn't react. The film makes clear he is not happy.

Cops arrive at the door and begin knocking. Ganz grabs the woman and brings her to the door at gunpoint, quietly telling her to delay them. She says she has to dress, but Ganz hits her with his gun. He enters the adjoining room, where Billy Bear and Rosalie wait.

Moving into the hallway, Ganz kills Vanzant and wounds Algran. Hearing gunshots while in the lobby, Cates tells the receptionist to call the police. He then proceeds up the stairs.

Reaching the top level, Algran tells him there are two gunmen taking the elevator down to the lobby. Cates heads back down the stairs, arriving in the lobby just as the elevator door opens. The men step out of the elevator as Cates opens fire.

Billy Bear fires, forcing Cates to duck, allowing Ganz to grab the receptionist as a hostage.

Ganz tells Billy to take Rosalie out in the open, because the cop won't risk wounding her. Billy tries it but Jack opens fire. Billy goes back into hiding.

The film makes clear that Ganz doesn't know what to do. Then Algran comes down the stairs, pulling the trigger of his now empty gun. Ganz tells Cates that if he gives him his gun, he won't be killed. Algran demands Jack not do it, but he ultimately

In 48 HOURS, San Francisco police detective Nick Nolte is forced to team up with convict EDDIE MURPHY....

does.

Ganz catches the weapon, compliments its feel and blows away Algran, before firing numerous shots at Cates, who leaps behind the main desk.

Ganz releases his hostage and runs out of the lobby and into an awaiting car being driven by Billy Bear.

At police headquarters, Cates is called on the carpet. The hooker says Ganz will give them a lot of trouble since the man obviously likes "shooting cops more than getting laid."

Cates goes over Ganz's background with a cop named Kehoe, then realizes the dead man found on the park bench is Henry Wong, a former member of the Ganz gang. Upon further investigation, he discovers that one of the gang members, Reggie Hammond, is still in prison, with six months left to serve on a three year sentence.

Cates goes to Hammond's cell, finding the man singing "Roxanne", wearing sunglasses and listening to a walkman. Cates is *not* impressed.

He questions the prisoner concerning Ganz and Henry Wong, but Hammond refuses to answer, insisting he won't screw over his old friends. Then he learns Ganz broke out of prison, and his attitude completely changes. He'll help Cates find Ganz, but he must first be released because he has a lot to protect.

Cates refuses and leaves. Despite the depicted action in the scene, the entire course of the film has demonstrated it's only a matter of time before he gives in and the two team up. Of course, since the prisoner is Eddie Murphy, it's clear he will do more than just sit in a prison cell for the rest of the film.

From Eddie Murphy's first appearance, the audience believes it's in for something special. Murphy carries an infectious sense of confidence that projects off of the screen.

In desperation, Cates forges some documents to have Hammond freed for forty eight hours, thus justifying the name of the film. At this point, the stream of one-liners begins. the film shows an instant rapport between the characters of Nick Nolte and Eddie Murphy.

Hammond leads Cates to Luther's apartment, and in return is handcuffed to the steering wheel while Cates breaks in. Luther takes a shot at him and runs into the street. Seeing Luther approach, Hammond whips the car door open, slamming it into him, sending the man flying over it while his gun ends up in Hammond's hands.

Hammond starts making wisecracks about the pain Luther is in, until he hears Cates warning him to drop the gun or he's dead. Looking over, he sees a gun aimed directly at his forehead. Hammond pleads with him to lower the weapon, and then smiles as he hands Luther's gun to the cop. Luther is arrested.

At the precinct, Cates calls Elaine while Hammond goes off to speak to a pair of prostitutes. The film is realistic, portraying a man who has been in prison for nearly three years.

Cates gets into another fight with Elaine, and she hangs up on him.

The dynamic duo then heads for the Mission District. They hope to find Billy Bear in a Country-Western bar named Torchys. Reggie bets Cates that they get a clue: his payoff will be permission to go and get laid. Cates reluctantly agrees, adding that if they get nothing, Hammond has to tell him everything. The film makes clear that Cates knows Ganz didn't break out without purpose. Cates is so confident Hammond won't turn up anything, he gives him his badge to aid in the performance. And *what* a performance it is.

This scene is Eddie Murphy's tour de force in *48 Hrs.* He identifies himself as a cop and starts tearing up the place when people don't cooperate. He threatens and insults the rednecks, shatters the large mirror behind the bar, kicks people around and establishes himself as *The Man.* Cates watches carefully, waiting for the moment he has to jump in. In the midst of all this, Reggie discreetly pockets a switchblade and a gun. Ultimately the bartender, not wanting his establishment damaged further, gives him the address of Billy's girlfriend in Chinatown.

In the street, Cates asks for the gun and knife from Hammond, who's impressed the cop saw him pocket them. From this point, the film makes it clear that an mutual admiration is growing between the men.

48-HRS-5251-3

They go to the girl's apartment only to be hit by a baseball bat swung by a pre-*Star Trek: The Next Generation* Denise Crosby. She then levels her gun at them. Cates points his gun back at her, until he eventually persuades her to lower her weapon. He asks about Billy Bear and is told she hasn't seen him, and probably won't because he owes her money.

Frustrated that a killer is using his gun and irritated Hammond isn't telling him everything, Cates gets into a fist-fight with his "partner". A terrifically sloppy slugfest follows as Hammond gets the best of Cates, and is then body-slammed into a row of garbage cans. Hammond looks like he's about to win, but Cates comes back and has nearly knocked him out when a squad car pulls up.

Cates identifies himself as a cop and they leave. Proceeding to a gas station, Cates prepares for another round. Instead Hammond finally tells him the truth, explaining that he's been waiting a long time for half a million dollars.

He and his friends hit a drug dealer during a sale and got away with the money, the kind of money nobody reports missing. Ganz "dropped dime" on Reggie, resulting in his arrest. Now Ganz, who was eventually also arrested, is after the money which Hammond hid.

The now united pair enter the parking garage in which Reggie's car has been for the past three years.

The building opens at 7AM the next morning. At that time, Luther, now out on bail, enters the garage and gets Hammond's dust-covered sports car. He drives off with Cates and Hammond in hot pursuit.

Luther parks the car, grabs the satchel of money and enters the subway system, with the duo still in pursuit. A tautly suspenseful screen chase sequence follows in which Ganz and Luther approach each other amongst the throng of commuters. Ganz catches sight of Cates and raises his gun, but a transit cop pulls out his own weapon and orders Ganz to drop it. Billy leaps out, fires and kills the man.

Luther runs off with the money with Reggie in pursuit. Cates chases Ganz and Billy Bear, who have Rosalie in tow. Ganz gets on a train and Cates raises his gun, but a pair of transit cops tell him to drop it, ignoring his claim to be a cop.

Disco temperatures soar with when EDDIE MURPHY meets Olivia Brown in 48 HOURS....

35

That night at Roman's bar, Reggie unsuccessfully tries picking up a variety of women. At the precinct, Kehoe looks at Cates and comments on the rumor that a soul brother kicked his butt. Cates denies it, then gets a phone call from Elaine. Unfortunately he infuriates her by cursing her out, thinking the call is from Hammond. They endure another fight. Kehoe mentions that a pal of his "from the Vice Squad" called.

Cates gets the number, calls and reaches Reggie at Roman's. He tells him where he is and Cates is already on his way when Kehoe reminds him Elaine is on hold.

He gets back on, and she tells him to screw himself and slams down the receiver.

By the time Cates gets to Roman's, Hammond is dancing with Candy. By all appearances, he's about to get lucky. Cates pulls him to the side, and is told that Luther is in the hotel across the street with an 8AM wake-up call. All they have to do is wait.

Hammond subtly displays a gun he picked up, but Cates doesn't even try to grab it. He's grateful Reggie called him rather than taking off with the money. He even apologizes for putting him down, noting he was just doing his job.

"Doing your job doesn't explain everything, Jack," says Reggie.

When Cates grudgingly concurs, the film offers the audience a nice character moment between the two major protagonists. To show his appreciation, Cates gives Hammond the money necessary for him to go across the street with Candy. The couple start to cross over, until he sees Luther leaving the hotel with the money. Hammond grabs Cates and the pair set off in pursuit.

Luther boards the city bus Billy is driving. In the back wait Ganz and Rosalie.

Luther approaches and gives him the money, asking Rosalie if she's okay. Apparently this isn't a question Ganz wants to hear, as he had promised he wouldn't hurt her. So he blows Luther away.

At that moment, Cates and Hammond pull alongside of them in Cates' rag-top Caddy. A spectacular shoot-out begins. What may be the first car-bus chase on film ensues. It ends with Cates' car smashing through a car dealership window.

At the precinct, Cates is harshly reprimanded by Captain Haden. The captain roars that five deaths have been attributed to Ganz, and yet Cates blew everything for the sake of a convict. He points out that this will mean a suspension and a hearing before the review board.

Cates roars out that Hammond has more brains than the captain will ever possess, and more guts than any partner he's ever worked with.

Cates and Hammond head outside to find the car which Cates had had impounded. They go for a drink, depressed over their inability to get Ganz. Moments later, Cates calls the squad room and talks to Kehoe, getting a report. The only news is that the bus has been found dumped in Chinatown.

Cates suggests to Reggie that they talk to Billy's girlfriend again. Reggie dismisses the idea until Cates notes they have nothing better to do with their time...except take him back to prison.

Entering the building on the heels of Billy's girlfriend, Cates pins her against a wall. He demands to know the whereabouts of Ganz and Billy. Once this is obtained they enter the apartment.

In the apartment, an armed Hammond finds Billy, who looks at his shaking gun, pulls a knife and starts to laugh. As Billy comes at him, Hammond shoots him twice.

Ganz leaps out, takes several shots at Cates and runs down the fire escape. Cates and Hammond follow from different points.

The film utilizes an interesting technique for effect at this point. The street fills with fog/steam as the action enters the alleys. Ganz, who has the satchel of money in one hand, trips Reggie, pulls his gun, holds him prisoner and screams out to Cates. A moment later, Cates, gun at his side, steps out of the fog, telling Ganz that he's not going to make it. Ganz laughs, because he's got the gun and the money, as well as a hostage.

Hammond tells him to blow Ganz's brains out, to which Ganz responds that the cop won't do it. Without a word, Cates fires and hits Ganz's shoulder, allowing Hammond to escape.

Ganz is more stunned by being shot than by the wound itself.

"You're done," says Cates. "End of story."

Ganz runs at him. Cates empties his gun and Hammond just stares on in shock.

At the film's end, Hammond has made love with Candy and met with Cates, who's taking him back to prison.

They talk about the money. Cates says it will still be in the car in six months when Hammond gets out. Reggie is surprised Cates doesn't want any of it, but he responds that taking money like that just isn't his style. On the other hand, he would welcome a loan so he can buy a new vehicle.

After they get in the car, Cates points out that despite the loan, if Hammond crosses the line, he'll bust his arse. He takes out a cigarette, and Hammond grabs his lighter and lights it, subtly putting the lighter in his pocket.

"Jack," Hammond asks, "both of us know I'm going to be an honest man from now on. But if I did decide to become a thief, what makes you think you could stop me?"

"Can I have my lighter back, Reggie?"

And with that they roar off into the night. The sound of the Busboys singing "The Boys Are Back in Town" fills the soundtrack.

As the credits roll, the audience is left feeling they have been through one hell of an adventure. Murphy and Nolte create screen magic together, acting as though they've known each other for years. The adversaries-turned-friends seem completely believable.

Walter Hill, who has directed a wide variety of films since this one, has never quite equaled its creative success. His every directorial move hit right on the money; the combination of humor and violence blending perfectly. For every violent action, the film offers a humorous re-action. The final product seems similar to the early Sean Connery James Bond thrillers. In both violence is accompanied by a dark sense of humor, justifying both violence and humor.

If any movie deserved a sequel, it is this one. It is unfortunate audiences would have to wait eight years to see one.

DAN AYKROYD   EDDIE MURPHY
They're not just getting rich...They're getting even.

TRADING PLACES

Some very funny business.

PARAMOUNT PICTURES PRESENTS AN AARON RUSSO PRODUCTION
A LANDIS/FOLSEY FILM · DAN AYKROYD · EDDIE MURPHY · "TRADING PLACES"
RALPH BELLAMY · DON AMECHE · DENHOLM ELLIOTT AND JAMIE LEE CURTIS
MUSIC BY ELMER BERNSTEIN · EXECUTIVE PRODUCER GEORGE FOLSEY, JR.
WRITTEN BY TIMOTHY HARRIS & HERSCHEL WEINGROD · PRODUCED BY AARON RUSSO
DIRECTED BY JOHN LANDIS   A PARAMOUNT PICTURE

□ Trading Places....

"....During the Depression, Hollywood spun some of its most glittering comedies from premises as farfetched as this. But *Trading Places*, a Reaganomics comedy that evokes those old feast-or-famine farces, seems more burdened by the mechanics of its plot than freed by it. The twists that ensue...are telegraphed so far in advance that you may feel that you, not Timothy Harris and Herschel Weingrod, wrote the script....The drolly preppy Aykroyd is more successful at creating a screen character than he has been before, though the suspicion remains that TV best suits his talents. No question about Eddie Murphy, though. John Landis' movie confirms what *48 Hrs*. suggested: Murphy is the most dynamic new comic talent around, a quicksilver quick-change artist whose rapport with the audience is instantaneous. Whether masquerading as an exchange student from Cameroon or indignantly complaining that his old street friends aren't using coasters with their drinks, Murphy is the movie's hottest—and funniest—commodity."

—Newsweek

"A rousing madcap comedy of the old school, *Trading Places* is chock-full of knock-em-dead opportunities for Dan Aykroyd and Eddie Murphy. Both, of course, are alumni of *Saturday Night Live*, and both are irresistible in director John Landis' ebullient spoof of big business at its baddest....Give some credit to Timothy Harris and Herschel Weingrod, authors of the uneven but inventive screenplay.....Murphy lording it in a mansion buttled by Aykroyd's sneering butler is consistently hilarious—with Akyroyd no less effective as the befuddle Main Line business whiz who eventually finds a heart-of-gold whore to help him fight back. When the guys start slipping into comic disguises, stylish fun almost gives way to standard *Saturday Night Live* shtick. But the movie always manages to get back on the track, seemingly guided by vintage Capra and Sturges ground rules, right up to a classic screwball-comedy sequence aboard a train loaded with good guys, bad guys and a lustful gorilla...."

—Playboy

THE CRITICS

EDDIE MURPHY and Dan Aykroyd 'trade places' as Murphy soars to riches and Aykroyd plunges into despair in TRADING PLACES....

THE CRITICS

"Trading Places....is reminiscent of the kind of 'classic' that turns up on TV at Christmastime, and it looks like a Christmas classic on a TV set that needs adjusting. It's drag. It's also eerily arch and static. Landis must thing that he's achieving a mock-thirties formal style; for the first hour he italicizes each scene, fixing it in place as if he wanted us to take an inventory of every detail. He seems to be saying, 'I'm smarter than this.' It gets to the point where you may want to stand up in the theatre and say, 'Yeah? Prove it.' The picture is pompous—the setups are so rigid I wanted to kick the camera to get it moving....Landis' timing is deadly—he makes everything obvious. And he doesn't do much for his actors. Aykroyd uses one fairly effective comic shtick: he plays rich by keeping his face tilted up, the nose high, sniffing purer air, like a snobby dog in a cartoon....Confusingly, though, he's less appealing when he's on the skids. Dan Aykroyd is all exteriors; he's big and beefy, and, inspired as he has often been on TV, he doesn't seem to have a strong personality....Eddie Murphy's new-style savvy carries *Trading Places*, but this is only his second movie and he's already just one step away from being in a niche. Murphy is like a child performer who's too accomplished. His cockiness is uncannily knowing; he gets to your reflexes, like those Vegas veterans who make you feel that you're enjoying them even while you're pulling man. This isn't a man possessed; this is a man who knows his audiences—he plays completely off their expectations...."*

—The New Yorker

"....[The screenwriters] have borrowed a little from Frank Capra, a bit more from Preston Sturges, who loved rags-to-riches and riches-to-rags stories, and a great deal more from a 1954 Ronald Neame movie called *Man With a Million*....John Landis directs crudely, slamming the story forward without much regard for credibility. Yet I laughed almost constantly and so did everyone sitting around me: The jokes on the rich, and on people who fall down dead before the rich, are good to hear at a time when the accumulation of wealth has been blessed by the current administration as the only virtuous human activity. Looking boyish, chubby, and, when close-shaven, in*white*, Aykroyd does his best to make Winthorpe human, but it's Eddie Murphy's movie. His talent for mimicry combined with his disbelieving smile make him the most sympathetic of con artists. The audience has taken this slick charmer to heart; he can get away with anything, and he knows it."

—New York Magazine

"....*Trading Places* makes it respectable again to enjoy one of our truly gifted comedians. Make that *two* of our truly gifted comedians, since Akyroyd's fellow *Saturday Night Live* discovery, Eddie Murphy, co-stars....It's all outrageously contrived, and only surprising restraint by director John Landis makes it work. The writing is superb, too, leaving the two funnymen free to do the most inspired textured portrayals either has managed in movies. Aykroyd is by turns infuriating and winsome....Murphy, meanwhile, adroitly and hilariously modulates his street wisdom and vulgarity into a high-class-white life-style. Getting out of such a convoluted, farcical plot on acceptable terms isn't easy. But Landis' climax works to perfection....One unseen star is Bonnie Timmerman, the film's casting director who has concocted one of the most entertaining cast chemistries in recent memory."

—People Magazine

"....How the two young men discover that they have been had and how they join forces to take revenge are the substance of *Trading Places*, one of the most emotionally satisfying and morally gratifying comedies of recent times. Perhaps because of an almost geometrically balanced structure, it has powerful persuasiveness when it moves the audience to the wilder shores of farce. Any movie that can punish a villain by involving him in a homosexual love affair with a gorilla and make the situation both plausible and risible is a picture to be reckoned with. *Trading Places* also makes Eddie Murphy a force to be reckoned with. It takes nothing away from Aykroyd's perfect prissiness as Winthorpe, or from Bellamy and Ameche...to say this. But Murphy, using his Tyrone Green character from *Saturday Night Live* as a sketch for a full-scale portrait, demonstrates the powers of invention that signal the arrival of a major comic actor, and possible a great star. He makes *Trading Places* something more than a good-hearted comedy. He turns it into an event."

—Time Magazine

THE CRITICS

45

After the somewhat startling critical and commercial success of *48 Hours*, everyone began wondering what Eddie Murphy would do as a follow-up. Apparently Paramount Pictures still was not convinced he could carry a film on his own. They teamed him up with Dan Aykroyd in John Landis' *Trading Places*.

The film opens with cuts throughout the city of Philadelphia, giving the audience a sense of the differences in life between the haves and have-nots.

We meet Lewis Winthorpe and are immediately put off by the rich, snobbish attitude he displays in every one of his early scenes. He goes to work at Duke and Duke (commodity brokers). When everyone bids him a good morning, he barely manages acknowledgements.

From there, the film cuts to the mansion of Randolph and Mortimer Duke, who head for their Rolls Royce. Their servants are lined up to greet them with a bright good morning, to which they give no response whatsoever. It isn't difficult to see from whence Lewis gets his attitude.

En route to the office, the Dukes, discussing an article in a magazine, heatedly debate whether heredity or environment shape a person. Meanwhile, they watch their computers and stock market reports. Mortimer wants them to sell their pork grind stock because the price is dropping, but Randolph holds him back from doing so. Ultimately the prediction Winthorpe made comes to pass, and the Dukes are several hundred thousand dollars richer as a result.

Once they arrive at Duke & Duke, Mortimer is approached by an apparently blind and legless man on a flat dolly, who begs him for money. Mortimer says he has no money for the likes of him, and a doorman rolls the beggar away. Inside the building, Mortimer discusses an upcoming orange crop report, while Randolph rambles on about the article pertaining to hereditary. Meanwhile, a butler comes over with morning refreshments and is given a five dollar Christmas bonus fr*both* of them.

Winthorpe comes over to get their signatures on the company paychecks. Randolph balks at a payment of $50,000 to a Clarence Beeks, a payment which confuses Winthorpe as well. Mortimer explains, reminding Randolph Beeks is conducting research for them. Randolph suddenly agrees. The Dukes tell Winthorpe he had best make an honest woman of their grand-niece. He promises to do his best. The con-

Street-wise con man EDDIE MURPHY tries to hustle Don Ameche and ends up a pawn in an elaborate game in TRADING PLACES....

versation abruptly ends and Winthorpe stands a moment like a child. Perhaps he waits for a simple "thank you" regarding the money he earned for them that morning alone.

Time passes. More time passes. Finally they dismiss him.

Without another word, he's gone.

Once departs, Randolph begins another conversation about hereditary and environment, using Winthorpe as an example.

Outside, the beggar tries to pick up a woman, until a pair of cops approach and give him a hard time. The beggar delivers a hysterically rambling speech about being a Vietnam veteran. Amused, the cops hoist him up and a second later, his legs lower. He thanks them and God for the gift of sight and the ability to walk which has suddenly been given him.

Continuing chants of praise, he walks away. Suddenly he bumps into Winthorpe as he's walking out of the Duke & Duke building. Winthorpe's briefcase drops to the ground, and the beggar, who the film eventually reveals as Billy Ray Valentine, good naturedly picks it up and tries handing it back. Winthorpe, instead of accepting the man's apology, calls out for help from the police, claiming he's being robbed. The cops run over and chase Valentine into the building.

Finally the beggar leaps off a table, landing on the floor with fifty guns aimed at his face by police officers. Valentine smiles and asks, "Is there a problem, officers?"

The Dukes walk into the room and are told by Winthorpe that the man attempted to rob him. Valentine insists the collision was an accident but is led away by the police after Winthorpe insists on pressing full charges.

When the others leave, the Dukes resume their ongoing debate. Randolph states that Valentine is a victim of his environment, while Mortimer claims it's hereditary; that no matter the opportunity offered to him, Valentine would turn out the same. Randolph believes that with the right chance, Valentine could run their company as well as Winthorpe does. He adds that if everything could be taken away from Winthorpe, he would take to crime like a fish to water.

They wager on the outcome, disclosing that they've engaged in similar such actions before.

At this moment the film delivers a clear sense of what filth these men really are, despite their trappings of sophistication. It is shocking to hear them contemplate the destruction of one man's life and the manipulation of another's just to win an argument.

At home, Winthorpe and Penelope go to the den to make love, while his butler, Coleman, is called by the Dukes. They spell out what they want done. He hangs up the phone and mutters, "What a scumbag."

Meanwhile, as Winthorpe undresses, Penelope states that she wants to have a party on January 2, but Winthorpe says that's the day the crop report comes out. It's his busiest day of the year. She's disappointed, but understanding. They begin their loveplay.

In jail, Valentine brags about being a karate expert as well as a pimp. The film offers a hysterical moment of screen comedy as he impresses a couple of teenagers and pisses off two older, rougher types. He's about to get his tail kicked when a cop comes over and tells him he's being released.

Shortly thereafter he steps out onto the street and is greeted by the Dukes in their Rolls Royce. Randolph asks him for a moment of his time while Mortimer holds up a bottle of whisky as an inducement for Valentine to join them. In the vehicle, the Dukes explain that they want to help culturally disadvantaged people. They want to give Valentine a job, a house, a car and money. After careful consideration, he accepts.

Valentine is brought into Winthorpe's house which is now to be his. He's told Coleman is his butler, and will do whatever he requests. Valentine tentatively accepts this state of affairs and goes off to take a bath. Mortimer tells Coleman to clean the young man's tattered clothing, because he'll need something to wear when he's returned to the ghetto. It's obvious Coleman is not enjoying the task.

Standing outside the Heritage Club—an exclusive club frequented by Duke & Duke employees, each more snobbish than the next—stands Clarence Beeks. He glances up at a window and gets a thumbs up sign from the Dukes. He nods and proceeds inside. Within the building, Mortimer voices concern that they may be pushing their luck using Beeks for this assignment as well as the crop reporter. Randolph dismisses his concern with a wave of his hand.

Meanwhile, Beeks bumps into Winthorpe, apologizes and a moment later introduces himself to the gathered executives as a security agent. He explains that there is a thief among them, currently holding cash stolen from the coat room; cash which had been marked. Everyone is asked to remove the contents of the jacket pocket of the man on their immediate left.

Winthorpe is found with the money. He protests his innocence, pointing out that he has no reason to steal. Dismay passes through the ranks as the Dukes voice the only vocal disapproval of his actions. The police lead him away.

Later, at the police station, Beeks bribes the sergeant in charge. Suddenly Winthorpe is found with PCP. It's apparent the book will be thrown at him for these trumped up charges.

Meanwhile Valentine is flaunting his new-found riches. He enters a bar he used to frequent and pays off a debt of fifty seven dollars. He then buys drinks for the house.

At the bar, he with his larger former cellmates who want to pick up where they left off. They remind him of his bragging about a limo and the "bitches" he owns. Valentine suggests they step outside. When they comply, they're stunned to see Coleman standing at the side of a limo. Enjoying the moment, Valentine invites everyone to his house for a party.

The ensuing party is too wild for Valentine's rapidly changing tastes. He is upset by cigarettes being put out on his Persian rug, heavy drinking, and people fornicating all over the house. Ultimately he disapproves of what they're doing to his home, and kicks everyone out.

Coleman notes, "Your friends seem to have had a good time." Valentine replies, "They aren't my friends, Coleman. They're just a bunch of freeloaders who treated my house like a zoo."

Bidding goodnight, he goes up to bed.

The film returns to the police headquarters. Penelope has bailed Winthorpe out of jail. It is obvious he has had the hell beaten out of him. He loudly proclaims that men wanted to have sex with him. Penelope tells him to quiet down, and then vocalizes the horror she felt that the man she loved—whose children she wanted to breast feed—is a drug dealer. He's been fired from Duke & Duke and is up for embezzlement charges.

Winthorpe proclaims his innocence, but Beeks has given a hooker, Ophelia, a hundred bucks. A minute later she kisses Winthorpe deeply, begging him for just a little fix. Penelope slaps him across the face and walks off in tears.

Stunned, he turns to Ophelia and asks why she did such a thing. According to his "friend," it was something that would get him off. She turns to indicate Beeks, but is surprised to see he's gone.

In a shared cab, Winthorpe tells Ophelia he'll pay her $50 for the $20 ride when they reach his home. They get there, but Coleman claims he doesn't know anyone named Winthorpe and slams the door in his face. He also says that if he doesn't go away, the police will be called.

They proceed to a bank where Winthorpe learns all of his accounts have been frozen. His credit cards are taken away and he is literally thrown out onto the street.

Ophelia gets in the waiting cab to leave but Winthorpe begs her to help him. She signals for him to approach the cab and when he does, she looks at his hands. Seeing the manicure, she senses the truth underlying his words. He gets in the cab and as they drive off to her home, they pass his limo. He and Valentine catch sight of each other and point an accusing finger. Then traffic moves again and they set off in opposite directions.

Winthorpe is lost, completely without direction.

Valentine arrives at the Duke & Duke building. Coleman tells him to be himself. "Whatever else happens," he adds, "they can't take that away from you."

Inside Valentine meets with Randolph and Mortimer who explain their business as commodity brokers. This scene culminates in a wonderful film moment as Eddie Murphy steps out of character to look at the camera, as if to say, "Can you believe these clowns?"

At Ophelia's apartment, Winthorpe is moaning and groaning about the turn of events. Ophelia, tired of his whining, tells him to shut up. She then spells out their deal: she will help him get back on his feet, and then he will pay her five figures.

At Duke & Duke, Valentine makes a suggestion regarding pork bellies, giving a streetwise response to the inquiries of the brothers Duke. Although Mortimer opposes the idea, they accept his advice. His prediction proves right in a sequence of the film that is hard to accept.

As the Dukes leave the room, Mortimer purposely drops his money clip. When the brothers arrive in the lobby, Mortimer is surprised to find Valentine running after him to return it. Randolph tells him to keep up the good work.

Mortimer's expression betrays his disappointment in Valentine's honesty.

Winthorpe shows up at the Heritage Club and finds that Penelope is now paired with Todd. Winthorpe, accepting this as best he can, assures them he's an innocent man, and will fight the charges. He just needs a bit of money for his defense.

He's surprised to find his friends all believe him guilty and don't want him around.

Dejected, he proceeds to a pawn shop. There he pawns a $7,000 watch for $50 because he can't produce a receipt to prove the watch isn't stolen. Before he leaves, he asks the pawnbroker how much a gun in the display case costs.

That night at a restaurant, Valentine eats dinner with the Dukes and a wide variety of rich people. He so subtly insults them, they don't realize he's laughing *at* them, not with them.

Winthorpe stands outside in the pouring rain, viewing the scene. He looks like a lost puppy with nowhere to go.

Dan Aykroyd delivers a terrific performance as Winthorpe, taking his character from a level of supreme arrogance to a point where his world has been stripped away from him. The actor forces the audience to feel sympathy for his character.

Eddie Murphy also proves his acting ability, taking the street-wise Billy Ray Valentine and slowly transforming him into a man of sophistication. His character finds it much easier to step into Winthorpe's world than Winthorpe does stepping into his.

Winthorpe returns to Ophelia's apartment burning with a fever. She nurses him back to health, trying to offer some comfort. The next morning, he's better, until he reads the Financial Journal and sees Valentine's face on the front page. Furious, he promises the Dukes a Christmas they won't soon forget.

At the company Christmas party, Winthorpe, dressed as Santa Claus, steals food and guzzles drinks for the satisfaction of repaying the Dukes in even a small way. Meanwhile, Billy questions the Dukes about a check issued to Clarence Beeks. They tell him not to worry about it. As they walk away, he overhears them talking about their wager, saying the other party is expected to turn to crime.

Valentine goes back to his office and finds Winthorpe placing drugs in his desk drawer. He tries to call security, but Winthorpe pulls a gun. The Dukes walk in at the same time as security, but Winthorpe holds them at bay. Randolph and Mortimer try to talk him into lowering the weapon, but he refuses. Instead, he moves into the main party area and waves the gun around, thrilled by the feeling of power as everyone cowers away from him. It's the first sense of control he's enjoyed since the nightmare began.

Moments later, the Dukes talk about the changes in Winthorpe. Valentine says that you can't be lenient to people like that, and that he knows from experience.

Moments later, a thoroughly drunk Winthorpe heads towards the lobby. Valentine goes into the bathroom to smoke a joint. He stands up on the bowl to blow smoke into the air vent. Then the Dukes walk in.

Assuring themselves that they're alone (Valentine crouches on the bowl so he won't be seen), they discuss their wager in detail. Mortimer then pays Randolph what he owes him for losing the bet: *one dollar*.

Randolph wants to know when they should bring Winthorpe back, but Mortimer emphasizes that he doesn't want him back, particularly after what he's done. They

53

also don't plan to keep Valentine around.

"Do you really think I'd have a niggar running our family business?" asks Mortimer.

"Of course not. Neither would I."

The Dukes note that the crop report is going to make the next year a very good one for them.

After they leave the room, Eddie Murphy stars in a wonderful scene for but a moment. The actor conveys a great deal in a very brief screen time. Upon hearing the phrase, "Do you really think I'd have a niggar running our family business?," his eyes bulge and dart about in shock. He projects the look of someone unexpectedly slapped viciously across the face. It's a credit to Murphy that he is able to say so much with a simple expression.

Winthorpe catches a bus home and Valentine follows in a cab a moment later. After Winthorpe gets off at his stop, a passing dog stops to urinate on his leg. Then a heavy rain begins.

Finally, feeling there's nothing left to lose, he pulls the gun from his pocket and puts it to his own head. He pulls the trigger, but nothing happens.

Returning to Ophelia's apartment, he locks himself in the bathroom. A moment later, Valentine arrives.

Awakening in his old bed, Winthorpe thinks the entire affair has been a bad dream, until he sees Valentine. He leaps on the man, intending to choke the life from him. Coleman and Ophelia pull him back, and Valentine quickly explains the wager between the Dukes, and the prize of one dollar.

Valentine tells a shocked Winthorpe that the best way to hurt rich people is to turn them into poor people. At that moment, a newscast comes on the television detailing information about the crop report, and that Clarence Beeks is in charge of security.

At that moment, they realize the Dukes hope to corner the frozen orange juice market by getting the crop report before it becomes public.

The next day, Valentine eavesdrops on all phone calls coming to either one of the Dukes. He finally intercepts one from Beeks, who arranges the exchange of money for a copy of the crop report. The exchange is to take place in New York.

Later, Beeks boards a train to the Big Apple on which a New Year's Eve costume party is taking place. He goes into a compartment and is joined by Valentine disguised as an African exchange student. They are then joined by Coleman dressed as a drunk Irish priest and Ophelia as "Inga from Sveden". As Beeks helps her with her knapsack, his attache case is quickly exchanged for an exact duplicate.

Billy takes the attache case to the men's room where Winthorpe photographs the contents.

Valentine then returns to the compartment and is joined a moment later by Winthorpe, now disguised as a fellow African exchange student.

This last disguise doesn't make a bit of sense. It isn't convincing and Beeks should surely recognize him.

Ophelia asks Beeks to get her knapsack so they can have a picnic. While he reaches for it, they exchange the attache cases again. Unfortunately Beeks catches them and exposes Winthorpe.

He leads them out of the compartment at hidden gunpoint. They go to the cargo car to a cage holding a gorilla. Jim Belushi follows, disguised as a gorilla for the costume party.

As Beeks is about to kill his captives, Belushi bursts in good naturedly, and is knocked out by Beeks.

This infuriates the caged gorilla, who thinks Belushi is a female, and it smashes a fist down on Beeks' head, knocking the man out. They decide to put Beeks in the cage.

Later the Dukes wait in a semi-lit garage. Valentine, in the shadows, tells them to slide the money over to him and he'll slide over the report. Unbeknownst to them, he has altered it.

Shortly thereafter, Coleman and Ophelia give Valentine and Winthorpe their life savings. The pair then take the train to New York's World Trade Center.

At this point the film can become confusing to laymen. The Dukes, having read their version of the crop report, tell their buyer to purchase as much frozen orange juice as possible, even if the price goes up. Actually they want to buy enough OJ to drive the price way up as other people begin buying as well believing "The Dukes know something." Apparently, and this is never explained in the film, Valentine and Winthorpe have already purchased OJ stock at the price of $102 and they start to sell when the price reaches $142. This causes the price to drop.

The Dukes observe this and realize the crop report they received must be wrong. They then try to get their man to sell, but all action is interrupted when the Secretary of Agriculture appears on television. He states there was no damage to the nation's orange crops the preceding winter. Everyone panics and tries desperately to sell as the price of the stock plummets.

At this point our heroes start purchasing stock. Ultimately Valentine, Winthorpe, Ophelia and Coleman become extremely wealthy while the Dukes are left penniless. The duo jokingly say that Valentine won the bet they'd made, with Winthorpe handing over the one dollar wager.

The exchange commissioner tells the Dukes that they need to remit $350 million by the end of the business day or their seats at the exchange will be sold off.

The strain of poverty is too much for Randolph, who suffers a heart attack. Mortimer doesn't even flinch, choosing instead to yell about the stupid article about hereditary and environment that started the whole affair.

Meanwhile, the film shows that Beeks, still in Belushi's ape suit, is being sent to Africa with the real gorilla. The gorilla seems very much in love with him.

Valentine, Winthorpe, Coleman and Ophelia lounge on an island somewhere, enjoying the good life. Winthorpe and Ophelia sun themselves on a private yacht, while Valentine, Coleman and their "dates" do so on the beach. Everyone lives happily ever after except the Dukes. But let's face it, they had it coming!

Trading Places is without a doubt one of John Landis' finest films, only occasionally sinking to the sophomoric humor of *Animal House*. It serves as a classic rags-to-riches/riches-to-rags Hollywood story. The two stars, along with Jamie Lee Curtis and Denholm Elliot, all shine. Dan Aykroyd gives his second best performance to date, following his Academy Award nominated role in *Driving Miss Daisy*. In his hands, Louis Winthorpe III goes through a true character change, from the snobbish, holier than thou rich man, to someone quite literally lost. Ultimately he becomes rich again while learning the lesson of the life he briefly lived.

Many critics point out this is Eddie Murphy's movie. As Billy Ray Valentine he takes the street-wise character he's become famous for and moves him to a new level of sophistication. In a sense, audiences would see even more of the first version of Valentine in Murphy's next starring role, *Beverly Hills Cop*. The actor deserves every bit of the credit he has achieved.

Best Defense....

"The East is the Middle East, where Lieut. Eddie Murphy is demonstrating a dubiously designed tank to dubiously inclined Arab buyers. The West is California, two years earlier, where Dudley Moore plays an engineer who gets into trouble by failing to give his undivided attention to making Eddie's lemon grow. And, yes, never the twain shall meet. But the poet's point is a poor comic premise. Though *Best Defense* provides both stars a few funny moments and offers some promising satirical ideas, its binary construction imposes a fatal jumpiness on it. Gloria Katz and Willard Huyck, who co-wrote *American Graffiti* and *Indiana Jones*, have proved they can do better. Huyck, the director here, will have to prove on some other occasion that he has a gift for being funny on film as well as on the page."

—Time

"Surprisingly, for a comedy about the weapons trade, *Best Defense* has not kept its eye on its targets. This is a tale about a little tank that couldn't shoot. But director Willard Huyck, who co-wrote the script with his wife, Gloria Katz, indiscriminately aims for whatever passes in front of his lens—without hitting a laugh.....The movie's major miscalculation is Eddie Murphy, who is billed as 'strategic guest star.' Playing an Army lieutenant manning Moore's tank in Kuwait, Murphy cannot unleash his put-upon-black routine. This time he's not the victim of discrimination; those humiliations are relegated to his two Middle Eastern trainees cum lackeys, who could be Arab descendants of the Three Stooges. Without a plot that suits his persona, Murphy looks lost. This misbegotten comedy is out of the *Deal of the Century* school of comedy; it's moral seems to be that the best defense is constant offensiveness."

—People

"The prospect of Dudley Moore and Eddie Murphy teaming their comic talents tantalizes the mind: how would two such disparate styles play off each other? Well, you can rest your minds, folks. They *don't* play off each other. In *Best Defense*, Moore and Murphy don't even appear in a scene together. Indeed, they hardly seem to be in the same movie.....*Best Defense*, already split in two by its dual story lines, lurches about desperately in search of a tone and a target. Is it a satire on industrial chicanery, a thriller, the story of a philanderer or *Stripes* goes to the Middle East? By the time the bullets start to fly in California and Murphy starts unloading rounds of ammo at Arabs, one knows all too well what this movie is: grindingly unfunny....."

—Newsweek

THE CRITICS

Eddie Murphy spent two weeks shooting his scenes for this film. The credits proclaim him a "strategic guest star" to Dudley Moore. Unfortunately tthis is quite truthful and it is obvious Murphy only appears to increase the box-office returns.

Moore portrays Wylie, a failure at the invention game and at romance. His various creations for the military are useless, and his romance with Laura is hitting rock bottom. One hope of salvaging his life remains: a souped up tank. Unfortunately, as everything else he has created, this device suffers its share of bugs to be worked out.

Another storyline runs concurrently in film time. In fictional terms it takes place two years later, as Landry (Murphy) demonstrates the tank for Arab allies in Kuwait. Disaster strikes and it looks like curtains for Murphy and company unless Wylie makes the proper corrections in the past. Only this can save future users of his weapon. Of course, he pulls it off.

Moore, who scored incredibly well with *Arthur*, is only mildly amusing as the harried inventor trying to keep his life together. Murphy, on the other hand, is given nothing more than fart jokes to make. The results are embarrassing.

Film-makers Gloria Katz and Willard Huyck tried to copy the formula they used in *More American Grafitti* presenting twin storylines, constantly jumping from the past to the present. In that film it was somewhat more successful, as the stories didn't really tie together. Here they treat the situations as though this was a time travel adventure similar to *Back to the Future* films. The protagonists have to go back to the past to rectify the present. The premise in this case simply does not make sense, and the film suffers for it.

Best Defense remains the one *true* blemish on Eddie Murphy's credits.

He's been chased, thrown through a window, and arrested.
Eddie Murphy is a Detroit cop on vacation in Beverly Hills.

BEVERLY HILLS
Cop

PARAMOUNT PICTURES PRESENTS A DON SIMPSON/JERRY BRUCKHEIMER PRODUCTION IN ASSOCIATION WITH EDDIE MURPHY PRODUCTIONS·A MARTIN BREST FILM
EDDIE MURPHY·BEVERLY HILLS COP·MUSIC BY HAROLD FALTERMEYER·SCREENPLAY BY DANIEL PETRIE, JR. STORY BY DANILO BACH AND DANIEL PETRIE, JR.
PRODUCED BY DON SIMPSON AND JERRY BRUCKHEIMER·DIRECTED BY MARTIN BREST·MOTION PICTURE SOUNDTRACK ALBUM ON MCA RECORDS AND TAPES

DOLBY STEREO
IN SELECTED THEATRES

A PARAMOUNT PICTURE

□ Beverly Hills Cop....

"To waste as precious (and expensive) a commodity as Eddie Murphy on something as flat and unprofitable as last summer's *Best Defense* is like spreading caviar on stale Wonder Bread. *Beverly Hills Cop* is no masterpiece, but it uses Murphy to maximum effect. At its best, the movie is exactly as brazen, charming and mercurial as Murphy himself, which is to say it is unimaginable without him......Behind Eddie Murphy's posture of confidence, however, is deeper confidence: the joke in *Beverly Hills Cop* is his utter and instinctive superiority to the 'by the book' cops he works with and outwits out West. He's so cool even he can't quite believe it. He's condescending and patronizing to everyone he works with. But instead of being offended by his wagger one is totally disarmed. Murphy is the audience's id, the good bad boy who breaks all the rules and ends up teacher's pet anyway.....He's one superhero who isn't defined by race or class. *He* can make a point of his color, but no one else does; he's equally at home in a Detroit ghetto or in a suite in a posh Beverly Hills hotel."

—Newsweek

".....Martin Brest's impudent cops-and-robbers comedy (from a screenplay by Daniel Petrie, Jr.) gives Eddie Murphy another golden opportunity to demonstrate his skill as a cheeky saboteur of the social order. While Murphy's moxie works to bring some smugglers and murderers to justice, the long arm of the law in laid-back Southern California is flexed rather languidly by Judge Reinhold and John Ashton, as a hilarious team of Beverly Hills undercover men who behave like a latter-day Laurel and Hardy.....Although slow getting started, *Beverly Hills Cop* is amiable and original—a funny clutter of character sketches that ultimately yield to Murphy's law and send you home feelin' good."

—Playboy

"Dirtier and hotter than Harry, Eddie Murphy is also the funniest screen cop since the Keystones. From the moment he flashes his radiantly lewd grin, this comedy caper is off and running.....Plausibility inevitably takes a back seat to fun, but a more incisive comic approach to police methods would have been welcome. Still, director Martin Brest has a quirky camera eye and a knack for details. Murphy, only 23, has never been more likable. He had star help in his first two movies (Nick Nolte in *48 Hrs.* and Dan Aykroyd in *Trading Places*), but he's kind of his own hill this time. Even when the plot misfires, Murphy comes out shooting from the funny bone—and it's bullseyes all the way."

—People

THE CRITICS

Not since the heyday of Sidney Poitier or Richard Pryor has a black actor touched a chord within movie audiences in the way Eddie Murphy has. Still, at the outset of his career, his studio, Paramount Pictures, was not confident enough in his abilities to allow him to carry a film on his own. They teamed him with Nick Nolte, fresh from his success in the TV mini-series *Rich Man, Poor Man* and the feature *The Deep* in *48 Hrs.*. For *Trading Places*, the studio execs paired Murphy with *Saturday Night Live* alumnus Dan Aykroyd. Both films hit big, grossing in the neighborhood of $100 million each, not a shabby neighborhood at all. They left one pressing question, though: how much of that box office had Murphy earned?

The critics singled him out in both cases, but what did the ticket buyers think? How well did the black star play in Peoria? Paramount decided to take a chance. They gave him the starring role in *Beverly Hills Cop*.

From the moment the film begins, the viewer is begins a cinematic roller coaster ride.

The fast-talking, always hustling detective Axel Foley uses a truck full of stolen cigarettes to lure a pair of criminals into his trap. When a squad car pulls up, all hell breaks loose as one of the men puts the truck into gear and takes off. The resulting chase, involving numerous police cars in pursuit, is incredible in its mindlessness. The truck plows through the Detroit streets, knocking cars out of its way like they're tinker toys. The police eventually force the truck off the road, but the driver escapes.

Axel goes to the police station and fellow officer, Jeffrey, tells him Inspector Todd is furious. The Inspector believes this is Axel's worst screw-up ever, particularly considering no arrests were made.

Moments later, Todd approaches and screams his lungs out at Foley for going undercover without authorization and using impounded evidence. Todd won't listen to explanations, declaring that if Foley screws up one more time he's going to find himself on the street.

That night, Axel heads home and finds his apartment door open. Withdrawing his gun, he enters. His best friend, Mikey Tandino, waits in the kitchen. A man with a criminal past, Mikey has been working for their mutual friend Jenny Summers as a security guard for the art gallery she manages. The men are overjoyed to see each other since Mikey had only gotten out of jail six months earlier. Missing Axel, he decided to come to Detroit.

During their conversation, he shows Foley ten thousand dollars in untraceable bonds he "borrowed" from someone in California. Axel doesn't want to know anything else about it.

When the men go out for drinks and to shoot some pool, the film conveys the deep friendship binding the ex-con and the cop. At the end of the night they return to Axel's apartment only to be attacked by two men. A man named Zack, wonderfully played by *Wiseguy*'s Jonathan Banks, questions him about the stolen bonds. During interrogation, Foley is knocked unconscious. Zack then tells Mikey never to return to California again. Mikey readily agrees. Just as it seems he's being cut a break, Zack punches him in the stomach and fires two shots into his skull.

Later, after the police arrive, Axel applies a compress to the bump on his head. An unhappy Inspector Todd notes that a convicted felon was murdered while hanging around with Axel, and that it was a professional hit.

Axel doesn't understand why the Inspector declares it a professional murder. Todd quickly explains the assailants didn't care about Foley or he would be in the meat wagon with his buddy.

Foley wants to investigate, but Todd refuses to grant permission. Foley requests vacation time, which Todd grants. He warns that if Foley butts into the case, it will be the longest vacation he ever heard of.

The camera cuts to Beverly Hills as Axel drives through the streets in his beat-up Nova. He takes in the sights and carefully watches the denizens of California. This sequence offers several quite funny moments. As Murphy reacts to what he sees, the audience is forced to consider how truly odd are the sights we take for granted.

Eventually Foley checks into the luxurious Beverly Hills Hotel. Since he has no reservation, he's unlikely to get a room, so he pretends to be a reporter for *Rolling Stone*. He accuses the hotel staff of racism and punishing him for *their* reservation screw-up. Naturally he gets his room.

Later, he goes to the art gallery where Jenny Summers works. The first person he encounters is Serge, played by Bronson Pinchot of ABC's *Perfect Strangers*. Axel tries to understand Serge's accent when the man begins talking to him. This scene, reportedly improvised on the set, is absolutely hysterical.

Then Axel is reunited with Jenny and tells her what happened to Mikey. He asks about the guy who hired Mikey and is told that their mutual employer is Victor Maitland.

Shortly thereafter, Axel, pretending to be a floral delivery man, bursts into Maitland's office. He tries to act friendly but immediately asks questions about Mikey. Zack, still reading a magazine, is instantly alarmed. Axel tells him about Mikey's death, and Maitland, played by Steven Berkoff, the villain from *Rambo: First Blood Part II* and the James Bond adventure, *Octopussy*, tries to express sympathy. He isn't very convincing.

Axel asks about Mikey's work, but Maitland alerts his security officers that Mr. Foley doesn't belong. A group of men carry Axel into the lobby and actually hurl him through a window.

A squad car pulls up an instant later and arrests him for possession of an illegal weapon and disturbing the peace.

"Disturbing the peace?" he asks incredulously as he's loaded into the car. "I got thrown out a .... window. What's the charge for being thrown out of a moving car? Jay walking?"

He's brought to the Beverly Hills police department, a perfectly clean and sterile environment equipped with state-of-the-art computers. Sergeant John Taggart and detective Billy Rosewood start filling out the paperwork on Axel, but it's only a matter of minutes before he and Taggart begin to argue. This culminates in Taggart punching him in the stomach.

Lieutenant Bogomil, witnessing this, steps out of his office and asks if Axel would like to press charges. He replies in the negative. Where he comes from, cops don't file charges against other cops.

Bogomil points out that they do everything strictly by the book. For starters they

would like to know why he didn't identify himself as a police officer. Axel replies that he's on vacation, but that he really can't wait to go back to Detroit. Bogomil says he has spoken to Inspector Todd, who pointed out that if Foley is working on the Tandino case, he will be brought up on charges and fired.

These sequences successfully convey the differences between Axel's normal habitat and that of Beverly Hills. The contrast is that between night and day. He's a man used to the gritty, darker side of police work, while California police are shown to be willing to let their computers do the dirty work.

That night, Jenny bails him out of jail, even though she's mortified he harassed Victor Maitland.

Axel reminds her of the stolen bonds, noting that when he brought up Mikey's name, Maitland decided to throw him out.

Jenny refuses to believe her employer could be involved with murder.

As they drive off, Axel looks in the rear view mirror and notices that Rosewood and Taggart are following them.

Axel and Jenny go up to his room, and he calls room service to order food for the cops in the car across the street. This creates a truly inspired screen moment.

Turning his attention back to Jenny, he says he's staying in town until he learns who murdered Mikey. In addition, he's thinking of going down to Maitland's warehouse to do some snooping around.

The camera cuts outside to deliver the pay-off Foley had set up with his phone call to room service. They actually deliver the food to Rosewood and Taggart, waiting in their car.

Meanwhile, Axel obtains a bunch of bananas, moves outside and shoves them into the unmarked car's tailpipe. The cops catch sight of Foley and Jenny getting into her car and driving off and Rosewood starts the car. The bananas do their job and cause it to stall out.

Axel and Jenny arrive at the warehouse and she reluctantly lets him in. When he finds coffee grounds, his suspicion is aroused. Before he can do anything about it,

An out-of-his-element EDDIE MURPHY chats with gallery employee Bronson Pinchot at an avante-garde California art exhibit in BEVERLY HILLS COP....

the warehouse door opens. They hide as two men bring a crate inside, open it and remove bonds. They place the bonds into a bag, seal the crate back up and reload it onto the truck.

The duo set off in pursuit. This is the most contrived sequence in the film. There is absolutely no reason for the men to do what they do except to quickly let Axel, Jenny and the audience know that Victor Maitland is tied into Mikey's death.

At headquarters, Rosewood and Taggart are reamed by Bogomil. He wants them to go back after Foley and warns that if he gets away again, they might as well not bother calling in.

Axel and Jenny follow the truck to another warehouse. This one holds items for the gallery until they clear customs. Foley tells her to go home and then scales a fence into the building. Once again he cons his way in, claiming to be an agent of customs doing security checks. Since security has become so lax, they are going to do a check on every crate, starting with the one just brought in. Obtaining the information he wants, Axel heads back to his hotel. He leaps into the back seat of the cop car and tries to strike up a conversation with Taggart and Rosewood. Foley is genuinely shocked to learn they were docked a day's pay each for losing him. He suggests they get something to drink and try to be friendly. Taggart refuses, and Axel responds by saying that he's going and they're going to have to follow him anyway. They finally agree, and go to the place of Axel's choice, a strip joint.

While everyone begins to relax, Axel hands an envelope with coffee grounds to Taggart. He doesn't understand their significance.

Before the conversation can progress, Axel catches sight of a pair of men wearing long coats and tells Taggart to prepare for trouble.

He asks Taggart to cover one of the men, while he goes to the one at the bar. Taggart doesn't know whether or not to believe him, but Axel states in all sincerity, "No bullshit this time." The men move off to their positions.

Pretending to be completely drunk, Axel approaches his target. The man shoves him away and pulls out a shotgun, as does his partner. Axel continues his drunk routine and disarms him with an elbow to the face. Taggart pulls out his own gun and presses it against the other man's temple.

The men are cuffed, and at last the film establishes a connection between Axel and the two cops.

At the police station, Bogomil again yells at the officers for entering an area outside their jurisdiction. Axel tries to take full blame, swearing the cops were in the strip joint only because they were tailing him. He even tries to give the duo credit for the arrest.

When Taggart tells the captain the truth, Axel is astounded they could take a perfectly good lie and ruin it. He departs and Bogomil takes the cops off the case. Instead Foster and McCabe are put on Foley's trail.

The next day, Axel sends food down to this duo and lets them watch him drive off. He parks outside Maitland's house, and the cops approach him, ignoring all his attempts to be friendly.

When Maitland's entourage leaves the mansion, Axel decides to pursue using a nearby traffic light to lose the officers. He follows Maitland to a private country club and once again cons his way inside, this time pretending to be Maitland's gay lover who wants to inform him he's contracted a strain of herpes.

The maitr'de prefers the message be delivered by Foley personally. Foley approaches Maitland's table, determined to ask questions. Zack approaches and tries to shove Foley, but instead is flipped onto a table covered with food. Zach is ready to explode, but with a wave of his hand, Maitland holds him at bay. Axel sits down next to Maitland and categorically states that he knows he had Mikey killed. And that he's going to be brought down.

Maitland delivers a warning, but they're interrupted by a pair of police officers who arrest Axel for illegal trespass and disturbing the peace.

At the police station, Bogomil wants to know why Axel keeps bothering Maitland. After a moment's hesitation, he tells the other cops about what happened to Michael Tandino, adding that he can't prove anything *yet*.

Bogomil considers this and asks to hear what he's got. Axel tells them Maitland is a smuggler. He saw the bonds which were bribed through customs without clearance, and found varying amounts of coffee grounds in the warehouse. Bogomil makes the connection that drugs are often smuggled in coffee grounds to throw off the dogs. His problem is there isn't enough evidence to connect Maitland, so there's really nothing they can do.

They're interrupted by the police chief. The chief wants Rosewood to bring Axel back to his hotel room so he can pack, and then escort him to the city limits.

Both charges of disturbing the peace have been dropped, but will be reinstated if Foley comes back into the city of Beverly Hills.

Meanwhile, Victor Maitland enters the art gallery and questions Jenny about Axel. He wants to know where he is so he can convey some information which might interest him. She claims she doesn't know his whereabouts. Maitland and Zack then leave the gallery, leaving a worried look on Jenny's face.

Elsewhere, Axel convinces Rosewood to go to Maitland's warehouse, where, as he learned the previous night, another delivery is scheduled.

They then heads for the gallery and Jenny tells them that Maitland had stopped by and was acting very strangely.

The three go to the warehouse. Axel tells Rosewood to wait in the car so as not to enter the premises illegally and jeopardize his job. Axel and Jenny sneak in, find a crate filled with drugs hidden in coffee grounds and are suddenly surprised by Maitland, Zack and several other people.

Outside, a panic-stricken Rosewood has seen the men enter the building.

Maitland cannot believe Foley's constant prying and is rather disappointed Jenny is involved with him. Maitland gives the order for Jenny to be brought out to the car.

A moment later Zack punches Axel in the stomach, noting that he should have killed him when he "popped your little friend."

Maitland and Zack join Jenny in the car and drive off,. Several other henchmen continue beating Foley up.

Rosewood enters the building, gun withdrawn, and shoots one of the men. This gives Axel the opportunity to take care of the other two. The duo race out of the building and into the unmarked car. Rosewood contacts the police station, leaves word for Taggart to check out the warehouse and disconnects the line.

They trace the radio call to Victor Maitland's address. Taggart sends Foster and McCabe to check out the warehouse, while he proceeds to Maitland's.

Once there, he tries to arrest Foley. Axel continues picking the lock to the front gate, stating that by the time they get a search warrant it will be too late for Jenny. Rosewood follows him inside and Taggart ultimately agrees to join them. Before they enter, he takes two shotguns out of the trunk.

The three move along the property.

The final ten minutes of the film present an outrageous, funny and suspenseful series of shootouts between the good guys and the bad. The police get reports of gunshots being fired at Maitland's address, and Bogomil decides to lead a team of numerous squad cars there.

At the mansion, the fire-fight results in Zack getting killed and Axel being wounded. Then Maitland pulls Jenny out of hiding, and aims his gun at her head. She elbows him and escapes, allowing Axel and the just arrived Bogomil to quite literally fill him with bullet holes.

Later, the police chief arrives on the scene and wants Axel arrested, but Bogomil steps forward and instantly concocts a lie that clears Foley of any involvement. Surprisingly, the chief, who knows he's full of crap, accepts this, telling Bogomil that his written report had better be ready by the next morning.

Finally, Axel bids farewell to Jenny and Bogomil and is ready to leave Beverly Hills, when he is joined by Taggart and Rosewood for a goodbye drink at a nearby bar. The film has now firmly established their friendship.

Surpassed only by *48 Hrs.*, *Beverly Hills Cop* provides Eddie Murphy with one of his most appealing on-screen personas. Axel Foley is a finely crafted role that gives Murphy the opportunity to tap into a seemingly endless repertoire of characterizations, while still delivering solid acting.

EDDIE MURPHY challenges Mark E. Corry to a game of pool in BEVERLY HILLS COP....

Axel combines a razor-sharp wit with finely honed police instincts. The latter rise to the surface when he is placed in an environment that couldn't be more alien to him than the surface of Mars.

The supporting roles are handled beautifully by John Ashton, Judge Reinhold and Ronny Cox. The trio of co-stars create and sustain believable relationships which develop as the story progresses.

Screenwriter Daniel Petrie, Jr. and director Martin Brest balance comedy and action. Their creative talents, combined with Murphy's comic timing, never allow the material to stray too far in either direction.

Unfortunately the sequel which arrived three years later couldn't light a candle to its predecessor.

EDDIE MURPHY IS BACK IN ACTION.

And all Hell's about to break loose.

THE GOLDEN CHILD

A MICHAEL RITCHIE FILM

PARAMOUNT PICTURES PRESENTS A FELDMAN/MEEKER PRODUCTION
IN ASSOCIATION WITH EDDIE MURPHY PRODUCTIONS, INC. EDDIE MURPHY THE GOLDEN CHILD
CHARLOTTE LEWIS CHARLES DANCE Music Score by MICHEL COLOMBIER
Co-Produced by DENNIS FELDMAN Executive Producers RICHARD TIENKEN and CHARLES R. MEEKER Written by DENNIS FELDMAN
Produced by EDWARD S. FELDMAN and ROBERT D. WACHS Directed by MICHAEL RITCHIE
A PARAMOUNT PICTURE

The Golden Child....

"*The Golden Child*, Eddie Murphy's first movie since *Beverly Hills Cop*, is one of those projects that make you wonder if there's any common sense left in Lalaland. In order to achieve the simplest end—i.e., getting Eddie Murphy in a funny situation—*The Golden Child* goes up, down and 8 million unnecessary miles all around. This movie is like a guy who wakes up and wants a cup of coffee. But instead of going to his kitchen and boiling some water, he takes a cab to the airport, flies to Colombia, hikes into the mountains, harvests a bag of coffee beans, charters a boat back home and settles down for his morning cup. The coffee tastes fine (and so do the laughs here), but you have to wonder if it was worth the effort. Is it *that* hard to come up with an appropriate vehicle for the most popular screen comic in America?.....The trouble with this plot is not so much that it's nonsense, filled with the same kind of overproduced special effects that were so out of place in *Howard the Duck*. Who wants to see the chambers of hell and giant winged devils and mountaintops collapsing in an Eddie Murphy movie? The priorities are backward: the backbone of the movie, from the surreal adventure to the utterly perfunctory love story that develops between Murphy and Lewis, feels like filler, while everything that actually *is* filler—the extraneous moments when Murphy gets to goof on the everyday stuff around him—are the only moments you laugh at and care about.....Murphy's comic reputation will emerge unscathed from *The Golden Child*, but he has to take part of the rap. Logic dictates that a star of his power had more than a little hand in the creative misdirection this venture takes. Did he have visions of himself as the Indiana Jones of funk?....What a wasteful comedy this is; it literally goes to hell to get a few off-the-cuff laughs."

—Newsweek

"There's no one better than Eddie Murphy when he plays the right guy in the wrong place (or vice versa). This movie, however, is so wrong there's no guy right enough to fix it. It would have been reasonable to expect more from Murphy under a director like Michael (*Fletch*) Ritchie. With a few good lines, Murphy could have held even *Heaven's Gate* together, yet Dennis Feldman's script makes even Eddie grind to a halt....As the moviegoer, your job is to find the film amid the smokescreen of special effects and busy lines. Good luck."

—People

THE CRITICS

The Golden Child was intended to be Eddie Murphy's change-of-pace film. He had brought his street-wise characterizations from *Saturday Night Live* to the screen in *48 Hrs.*, altered it a notch in *Trading Places*, flopped in *Best Defense* and came into his own in *Beverly Hills Cop*. He had considered a starring role in *Star Trek IV: The Voyage Home*, but opted, instead, for *The Golden Child*. The film was planned to bring him where he had not gone before, into the realm of fantasy, the supernatural and special effects.

The film begins at a temple in Tibet as monks revel in the presence of the Golden Child, the youth who serves as their divine leader. This sequence intercuts with one of a caravan of bizarre looking travellers transversing a blizzard to reach an unknown objective.

At the temple, the Golden Child touches a dead bird, which miraculously returns to life and flies away. At that moment, the doors burst open and the travellers arrive, murdering many of the monks. The Golden Child is encased in a steel cage.

One of the men slips and the child touches his hand, resulting in the man moving to defend him. He turns on his master, Sardo Numspa, who vanishes and reappears a safe distance away. Numspa kills the man. Then the imprisoned Golden Child is carried out.

The bird he brought back to life flies out at the same time.

This pre-credit sequence is both mysterious and exciting, quickly capturing the imagination. It tantalizes the viewer by presenting a variety of dramatic clues which beg to be explored.

Over the credits, Chandler Jarrell hangs posters of missing children on telephone poles, seeking information concerning their whereabouts. In this musical montage, the audience sees him interacting with and observing the locals, obviously amused by the sights much as Axel Foley was in *Beverly Hills Cop*. Unfortunately, since this is the city where Jarrell lives, it really doesn't seem appropriate.

It is common knowledge that comedic moments were added to the film after it had completed shooting to make it more similar to what Murphy had done before. It's likely these moments are among them.

THE FILMS OF EDDIE MURPHY

Jarrell next appears on a local cable TV show as he tries to express his concern regarding the whereabouts of a young girl named Sheryl Mosley. Unfortunately he is constantly interrupted by the show's host, who asks the most inane questions imaginable. Jarrell eventually takes the microphone, puts his message on the air and departs.

Shortly thereafter, while he is playing basketball with neighborhood children, he is approached by the beautiful Mei Lei, who seeks his aid in finding the Golden Child. She adds that he must help her, as it is his destiny as the chosen one. Jarrell laughs this off, saying that it's her destiny to seek psychiatric help.

The following day, Jarrell is at the scene where Sheryl's body has been found. Strange inscriptions have been painted on the walls in blood. On the stove, he finds a pot filled with oatmeal and blood.

As Jarrell begins investigating her death, Mei Lei constantly and mysteriously appears. Finally he has coffee with her at a local diner. She looks at the photos taken on the scene and deduces the Golden Child was in that house. The inscriptions are incantations of evil designed to prevent the Golden Child from astrally projecting himself.

Jarrell still doesn't believe a word of this, but she points out that if he finds her killers, he'll find the Golden Child.

Mei Lei brings Jarrell to the basement of a ship, where they talk to a mysterious woman who remains behind a wall of rice paper. She explains that the Golden Child is the source of compassion in the world and that if he dies, so will all of man's compassion, resulting in the world becoming hell. He is their only hope.

Jarrell asks about the blood and oatmeal mix he found, and is told that nothing from this world will harm the child, but if he were to take anything impure into his system, he would become vulnerable.

The film suffers from a severe defect in this scene. Murphy takes the information so lightly, the audience follows suit. While being skeptical is understandable, he's *so* facetious it causes the viewer to ignore pertinent information. The scene is one indication two genres have been forced into one for this film.

Outside, Mei Lei explains that the woman behind the screen is over 300 years old, and that one of her ancestors was raped by a dragon. For this reason, she knows a great many things about the universe, and the Golden Child in particular.

She drives Jarrell home and he tries to get her to come upstairs, which she refuses to do.

The camera cuts to a warehouse where the Golden Child is kept in his cage, surrounded by evil symbols and men chanting incantations.

One man shoots rocks at the child, but the golden one merely raises a hand and deflects them. Seeing that the man is fascinated by his abilities, the Golden Child causes a discarded Pepsi can to stand up and turn into a dancing figure. This amuses the guards.

Suddenly, Numspa stamps down on the can, telling the child that he *will* eat. When Numspa departs, the child subtly removes a flower from his pocket and eats one of the leaves.

The film then shifts locations to Jarrell's apartment with Mei Lei still in her car. Cutting back to the child's point of view, the film shows one of the guards asleep. This allows the youth to astrally project himself.

Again, the camera returns to Jarrell's apartment, as he looks out a window and sees the glowing image of the child. The image unleashes the bird seen earlier. An anonymous phone call follows, which leads Jarrell to the house Sheryl had been taken to by bikers.

Upon arriving, he tells Mei Lei to stay in the car and that if there's a problem, she should get the police.

He sneaks into the house as the bikers drink beer and watch MTV. He pulls his gun, but is taken by surprise and tied to a wall.

Mei Lei dispatches several of the bikers including one by swinging on a water pipe to deliver a kick. The pipe bursts and sprays water. It is obvious this incident with the bursting pipe occurs with the sole intention of highlighting the shape of the actress' breasts.

She frees Jarrell, who takes care of several other bikers. He questions one of them about Sheryl and is told they sold her to Tommy Tong for a case of cigarettes and some pork fried rice. Tong needed her blood for a deal he'd made with the devil.

Jarrell, upset by the "selling" of Sheryl, decks the guy. Murphy conveys sincere feeling to the audience in this sequence.

The duo go to Tong's restaurant, where the man, armed with swords, leaps out at them. Once again, Mei Lei saves the day. They then pursue the man into the alley where a rat runs in front of Tong and transforms into Sardo Numspa.

He kills Tong and Jarrell and Mei Lei find the mutilated body. She concludes they may be dealing with demons.

At his headquarters, Numspa begins praying to the Devil, and suddenly descends into the pits of hell. The voice of Satan tells him to move the child before the chosen one arrives, adding that Numspa should obtain a sacred dagger, not of the Earth, to kill the youth.

To get the dagger, he is to tell Jarrell he will exchange the child for it.

At this point, the film fails to make sense. The movie has shown Numspa's incredible abilities in action. Why doesn't he simply appear where the dagger is and remove it himself? After showing his powers, it's illogical to include Jarrell in this extra step. Without it there wouldn't be much story to tell, though. Perhaps the dagger is in a place evil people cannot go?

That night while he sleeps, Jarrell witnesses a surrealistic dream in which he is with Numspa and his minions in front of a live studio audience. Numspa tells him he'll exchange the child for the dagger, and scars Jarrell's arm with his nail to prove the experience was most definitely real after he awakes.

Jarrell humiliates some of Numspa's people in front of the audience, then makes a run for freedom. En route he finds Mei Lei dressed sexily and tied to a wall with toilet paper. He frees her and she responds very romantically, very much in need of his protection. The minions attack, but Jarrell springs up in his bed, awakened from the dream.

He immediately examines his arm, and discovers the scar.

Jarrell and Mei Lei return to the woman behind the screen with what they know. She tells them the dagger must be obtained in Tibet and kept from Numspa. This is more than Jarrell can cope with. He feels things have gone too far.

That night, Mei Lei drops him off at his home and invites herself up. The next morning, she talks about Tibet and he finally agrees to go with her.

The camera cuts to a shot of the child being moved, and then to Tibet.

On arrival, the mystical bird leads him to an old man selling medallions. This man, who apparently can't speak English, takes a one hundred dollar bill from Jarrell's roll of money and then gives him the wrong medallion rather than the one of his choice. Jarrell explains that he's taken the wrong bill, when the man surprises him (and the audience) by responding in perfect English, "You're breaking my heart, ass wipe!"

Upon hearing this, Jarrell hoists him up and the man throws his money into the air. Jarrell turns around to see where it went, and when he turns back, the old man has vanished, leaving only his clothes in Jarrell's hand.

Confused, Jarrell meets up with Mei Lei. Together they row across a river and travel up lovely snow covered mountains.

Jarrell and Mei Lei arrive at the temple shown at the beginning of the film. The monks sit seemingly awaiting their arrival. Mei Lei asks for the dagger, but the leader, actually the man that ripped Chandler off earlier, tells him to ask for it. He does so, and is told that only a man of pure heart will be able to wield the knife.

Jarrell must pass sacred tests, including walking over a bottomless pit on the tops of wooden posts. The film generates suspense in this sequence, as Jarrell must put away his skepticism and for the first time truly believe in what he is doing. Once he does, the dagger is his.

At this moment, Eddie Murphy delivers a convincing acting job, reacting to the horrors around him and the possibility of plummeting into the pits of hell. At last he stops winking at the audience. This results in some of the film's most effective mo-

ments.

They go to the airport and Jarrell places the dagger in an obnoxious man's jacket. When the man is stopped by security, Jarrell jumps into the situation, claiming to be a member of the American Artifact Agency. Giving the type of performance he made famous in *Beverly Hills Cop*, Murphy successfully cons his and the dagger's way through security.

They arrive at Los Angeles International airport and Jarrell is approached by Numspa and a pair of police officers. Sardo claims Jarrell had stolen his property. Taking advantage of the situation, Jarrell begs to be placed in jail.

Numspa pulls Sardo to the side, and points out that if Jarrell's arrested, God knows when he will be able to get the knife out of evidence. Jarrell says that if Numspa brings the child, he will exchange the knife. Then he turns his attention to the cops and claims that his "brother" has forgiven him.

This is another moment in which Murphy can deliver one of his patented routines. At the core of this scene lies the aforementioned problem of why Numspa doesn't simply appear wherever the knife is and take it. Again, perhaps the knife cannot be taken by evil only delivered to evil by good. This is thin logic indeed.

That night, minions of Numspa show up to kill the duo, but Mei Lei provides more than a helping hand to save Jarrell. Numspa appears and is about to fire a crossbow at Jarrell, but Mei Lei leaps in front of the bolt and receives it in her back. She slumps to the floor, and Jarrell is absolutely overcome with emotion. Numspa departs.

Eventually Jarrell brings her body to the woman behind the screen. He is told the Golden Child can restore her to life as long as sunlight touches her body. Angered at all the riddles, Jarrell pulls the screen aside and is shocked to find that the woman is truly half-dragon. He learns that Numspa cannot kill the child until dark, so Jarrell has at least that long.

Meanwhile a dead butterfly lying in the child's cage is touched by him and brought back to life. Then he touches the hand of one of Numspa's henchman, and a smile crosses the man's face. He kicks aside the bowl of oatmeal and blood.

The camera moves outside, where Jarrell is driving his car, following the bird that has appeared throughout the film. Eventually the bird leads to a house which Jarrell enters.

He kills one of the henchmen, but another is about to shoot him with a crossbow when the converted man saves his life. The man then leads him to the cage containing the Golden Child. Together the man and Jarrell pry open the cage, allowing the child to escape.

Jarrell tells the man to watch the child while he goes to kill Numspa with the dagger. Unfortunately he doesn't expect Numspa to transform into a winged creature from hell. This drains him of all resolve and Jarrell hustles the child into his car, but he doesn't have the keys.

The child uses his magic to start the car and fasten his seatbelt. Jarrell tears out with the flying Numspa in close pursuit. The creature eventually drives them off the road, and they run through a series of abandoned buildings.

Numspa burrows through the ground and approaches the duo, out for blood. A fierce battle follows as the very walls start to collapse, apparently crushing Numspa to death while Jarrell escapes with the child.

They make it to the basement of the shop, where the lifeless Mei Lei lies. As they approach, a still very much alive Numspa bursts through the wall, ready to continue their battle.

He grabs the dagger and attempts to stab Jarrell, but the blade strikes the medallion bought in Tibet, which sends the weapon flying. The child then uses his telekinetic abilities to shift the knife into Jarrell's hands. Moving quickly Jarrell drives it into the winged Numspa, finally killing the creature.

It is this sequence of events that drives home the central failure of the film. If the villain can now grasp the dagger without the consent of the hero, he should have been able to take the dagger at any time. The possibility that good is required to voluntarily relinquish the dagger to evil is lost.

The Golden Child touches Mei Lei and she comes back to life.

At film's end, Mei Lei plans to take the Golden Child back to Tibet and return to Jarrell in two weeks time. All indications are that the two will eventually marry.

Many critics felt that the last fifteen minutes of *The Golden Child* were completely incongruous with an Eddie Murphy film. Yet, despite some poor mattes, these climactic sequences are really quite splendid because the actor no longer appears disinterested in the events around him.

Instead he uses his famed comedic talents to deliver something completely unexpected, in character and believable.

AXEL FOLEY
IS BACK.

BACK WHERE
HE DOESN'T
BELONG.

EDDIE MURPHY
BEVERLY HILLS
Cop II

THE HEAT'S BACK ON!

PARAMOUNT PICTURES PRESENTS A DON SIMPSON/JERRY BRUCKHEIMER PRODUCTION IN ASSOCIATION WITH EDDIE MURPHY PRODUCTIONS, INC. A TONY SCOTT FILM
EDDIE MURPHY · BEVERLY HILLS COP II · JUDGE REINHOLD · JÜRGEN PROCHNOW · RONNY COX · ALLEN GARFIELD · EXECUTIVE PRODUCERS ROBERT D. WACHS AND RICHARD TIENKEN
SCREENPLAY BY LARRY FERGUSON AND WARREN SKAAREN · STORY BY EDDIE MURPHY & ROBERT D. WACHS · BASED ON CHARACTERS CREATED BY DANILO BACH AND DANIEL PETRIE, JR.
PRODUCED BY DON SIMPSON AND JERRY BRUCKHEIMER · DIRECTED BY TONY SCOTT · A PARAMOUNT PICTURE

THEATRE SPACE

□ Beverly Hills Cop II....

"......The movie suffers from sequel slippage, with a plot so skimpy it could be printed on a pinhead with room to spare.....Murphy loyalists probably will not care, and director Tony Scott keeps the action fast, loud and just about nonstop....For me, the second time around is pure hype without much hilarity, but why cite logic against Murphy's law? Stay tuned for *B.H. Cop III*."

—Playboy

"......Everything anyone thinks might possibly have contributed to [the success of the first film] is presented and noisily accounted for the second time around: the pounding rock score with the volume turned up to brain-damage level; the incomprehensible plot; the music video montages of the good life in Beverly Hills alternating with sudden descents into motiveless and entirely humorless violence; the none-too-subtle maneuvering to bring Murphy into contact with variously dim figures who can be run over by his motor mouth; the police colleague-foils....whose chief function is to shake their heads bemusedly over Murphy's improvisational nerve and witty, if occasionally obscene, sayings. Above all, no attempt has been made to expand Murphy's character.....There is an inherent problem about any sequel that too slavishly duplicates the style and substance of its predecessor; it cannot deliver the delight of discovery that the original provided. Axel made a swell first impression, but he is still living on it, perhaps not yet a bore, but not quite as fascinating as he once promised to be...."

—Newsweek

"It's not easy to make a successful sequel to one of the largest grossing films of all time. But comic actor Eddie Murphy pulls it off without a hitch in his latest money-maker, *Beverly Hills Cop II*....One of the things that keeps audiences coming back for more of Eddie Murphy's Axel Foley is knowing this streetwise, cocky, Black man is going to give the uppercrust, genteel folk of Beverly Hills a run for their money....The movie rolls quickly and there is never a dull moment, with one rib-tickling line, shootout or chase scene after the other. With the success of Murphy's latest silver screen venture, chances are moviegoers haven't heard the last of Axel Foley."

—Jet

THE CRITICS

Too many sequels fail to take the characters and premise of the original film and evolve in new and different directions. More commonly sequels merely offer an audience more of the same, only bigger and noisier. There are a few examples of the first, including such innovative sequels as *Godfather II, Lethal Weapon 2* and *Rocky III*. Unfortunately the latter includes more titles than could possibly be listed here, including *Beverly Hills Cop II*.

The film begins excitingly enough with a jewelry store heist led by Karla Fry. They clean out the store in exactly two minutes and take off.

The film shifts locales to Detroit, Michigan, and we find Axel Foley in the midst of another set-up. This time he's after the makers of phony credit cards. He has gone undercover as a fabulously rich individual, whose trappings including $500 suits and a Ferrari.

Axel meets with his contact and orders 2,000 blank American Express cards which he needs in three hours.

In Beverly Hills, Captain Bogomil jogs past an oil refinery, stops and runs his hands through some of the sand. Something most definitely isn't right with it, but that isn't explored as the camera cuts to Bogomil's office. He calls Axel Foley, now returned to his own precinct. Photos on Bogomil's desk show that he, Axel, Taggart and Rosewood have remained friends.

In Detroit, Axel answers his phone and is delighted to hear his friend's voice. Bogomil cancels a fishing trip they were planning. Axel notes this is no problem as he is very busy with his current assignment.

Axel sets off for his meeting and the camera returns to Beverly Hills. Bogomil, Taggart and Rosewood are discussing an alphabet criminal whose first target was the jewelry store.

At that moment Chief Lutz walks in, demanding that the three come to his office. The film quickly conveys that this new police chief has fired every cop who served under his predecessor, except for the three of them. The trio now refer to each other on a first name basis.

In his office, Lutz yells at Rosewood for contacting the F.B.I. regarding the alphabet crime, and at Bogomil for allowing him to do so. Bogomil is suspended for failing to supervise his own men. Taggart and Rosewood are placed on traffic detail.

These opening scenes illustrate the many changes in the Beverly Hills police department since the events of the first film. The changes range from the way cops talk to each other right down to the once sterile environment now being a smoke-filled, gritty place to work. While it's understandable their experience with Axel taught them to loosen up a bit, how does one explain the rest? It seems director Tony Scott wanted to lend a look of his own to the station, but it just doesn't make sense that things could so "fall apart."

An angry Bogomil gets into his car and pulls away as another car falls into place behind him before passing. As he continues driving, he sees the car pulled over to the side, its hood open and a statuesque brunette standing beside it. Being a good soul, Bogomil offers to help.

The woman hands him an envelope with the letter "B" written on it just as someone shoots him from a passing car. He reaches out to the woman and pulls off her wig, revealing that this is Karla Fry.

She, too, fires her weapon at him. They then leave the man as dead.

In Detroit, Axel shows up for his meeting, but the man isn't there yet. He goes into his office and starts flipping through a magazine until the television new's "L.A. Desk" reports that Bogomil has been shot.

Axel calls the police department in Beverly Hills and is transferred to the hospital. He talks to Bogomil's daughter, Jan.

Rosewood gets on the phone, telling him that things have changed since he was last there and that it doesn't seem likely he and Taggart will be given the case.

Axel has to suddenly hang up when his target arrives. The man is accompanied by his nephew, who just happens to be one of the guys involved in the cigarette deal that opened the first film. The men begin exchanging insults, culminating in Axel leaving the deal until a future time when the man isn't around.

Going back to his precinct, Axel tells Jeffrey he has to go out of town and wants him to drive the Ferrari for a few days and be his undercover partner. Jeffrey is delighted.

Axel then goes to Inspector Todd, who wants to see some arrests for all the money the department has fronted him. In fact, he wants to see results in three days or he's going to "grind [his] ass into dog meat." Axel swears he's going to go deep, deep, deep undercover, so no one is going to be able to find him.

Axel flies to California and heads straight for the hospital. He convinces Taggart and Rosewood to show him the letters from the alphabet criminal,. They agree to meet at the precinct in one hour.

Axel consoles Jan Bogomil, then departs. At this point, the film slips into repetition as Axel takes in the local sights while the soundtrack blares. This time it's no longer fresh and innovative as it had once been.

Then, instead of talking his way into the Beverly Hills Hotel, he stops at a mansion where renovations are being made while the owners are away for a week. He convinces the foreman that the plans to the house have been changed, and that it will take several days for everything to be worked out. He tells him his men might as well go home. They do, and Axel finds himself living in a mansion.

At the precinct, Axel goes over the evidence with Taggart and Rosewood, pointing out that the bullet casings found on the scene aren't even being made any more and so must be custom. It's amazing no one else had figured this out until Axel arrived.

Chief Lutz walks in and Axel claims he's a psychic named Johnny Wishbone. Lutz tells him to leave, which he does. The man then tells Taggart and Rosewood to get on traffic before they're fired.

Foley meets them outside and all agree to solve the crime together.

To investigate the bullet casings, Axel goes to a private gun club and pretends to be a courier dropping off a paper bag filled with explosives. The receptionist stupidly accepts his con-job and allows him to drop the package off himself. Besides being silly, this particular scam is similar to the herpes story that got him into the private social club Victor Maitland was lunching at in the first film.

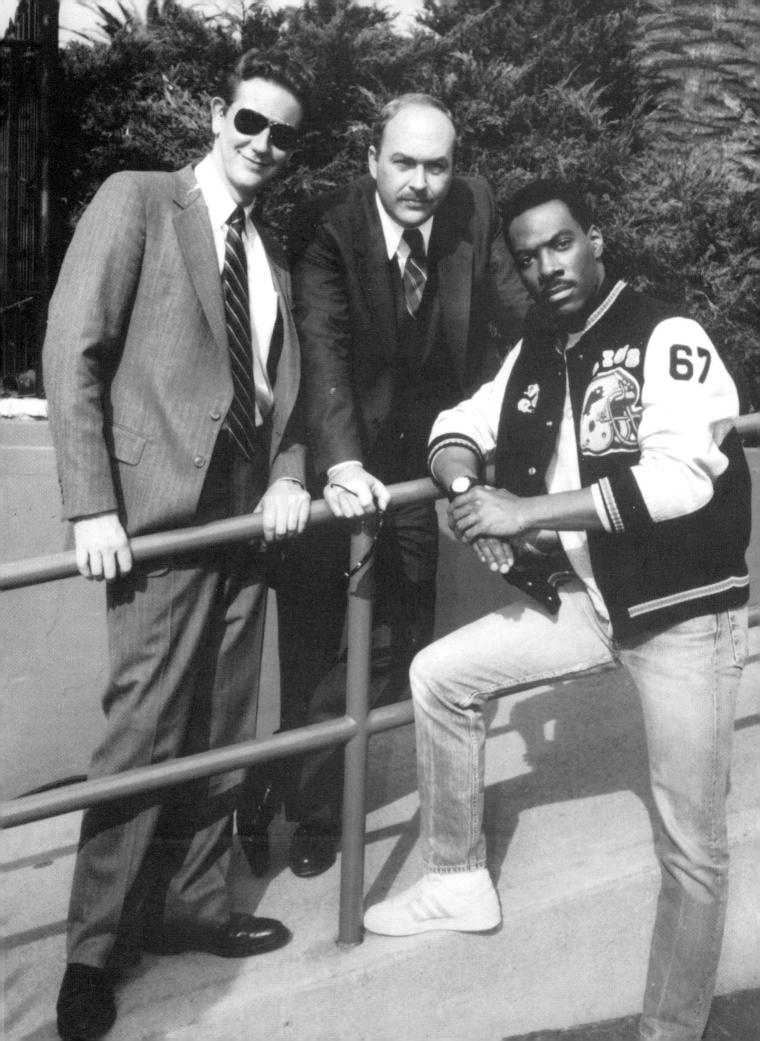

He makes his way into the club and asks questions about the bullet casings. The questions cause Karla Fry to come and talk with him for a moment.

Then, left alone in the shooting range, Axel discards the practice gun designed to be used on the projection screen in front of him and fires several shots from his gun, ripping the screen wide open.

Meanwhile, Karla goes to see Maxell Dent. She tells him about the casings, which were made for fellow employee Chip Cain, and leaves as Cain walks in.

Dent wants the "C" and "D" crimes to be pulled off without a hitch. They need to pay ten million dollars to someone named Thomopolous by Friday. Then he chastises Cain for the shells which were found, and the man in the club asking questions.

Cain goes down to the shooting range and finds Karla firing shots at a miraculously repaired screen.

He offers to make Axel an honorary member and asks where membership material can be sent. Axel gives him the address of his "home" and departs.

A moment later, Cain tells two of his hitmen to take care of the cop. One of them asks for a light, and he gives the man a pack of matches.
Axel meets Taggart and Rosewood outside the club. Then Axel goes to Bogomil's house rummages through the man's files, obtaining information on an establishment called 385 North, as well as articles on oil prices dropping.
He meets with Jan, and asks her to use all her connections at the insurance company she works at to find out what she can about Maxwell Dent.
Before he leaves, Axel finds a pair of Bogomil's running shoes, encased in dirt coated with oil.
Later Rosewood and Taggart arrive at the address Foley gave them and find him floating in the pool on a small raft.
The trio eventually depart to 385 North, a private strip-club. Axel cons the owner and fellow patrons into believing Taggart is former president Gerald Ford, and they gain admission. Axel discovers that the owner of the club is a man named Thomopolous, who Taggart identifies as the biggest arms dealer on the West Coast. With that revelation they leave. This scene does little more than get another strip-joint into the film, presumably because the original had one.

Judge Reinhold, John Ashton and EDDIE MURPHY are reunited on the trail of a gang of international thieves....

They step outside and exchange fire with Cain's men. The killers' car flips over, but the people within escape. Axel picks up the book of matches Cain had previously given the driver.

They go to Rosewood's apartment. It's obvious Billy has developed a Rambo/ Sylvester Stallone fixation, with posters and weapons all over the place. Utilizing the fumes from crazy glue, they lift a fingerprint from the matchbook and use the police computers to match it with those of Chip Cain.

Axel recognizes him from the gun club.

They make it their next stop, despite the fact that it's closed. Once again demonstrating expertise all other cops seems to lack, Axel shows his two friends how to use chewing gum to bypass the club's alarm system.

They enter Dent's office, and find a piece of paper with map coordinates on it in the desk drawer.

The next morning, they plug the coordinates into the computer and come up with the City Deposit. This must be the scene of the upcoming "C" and "D" crimes.

Switching locales, the film shows Karla and her people breaking in through the ceiling. It then intercuts to the trio en route to the scene and back again as the group starts to rip the place off.

Axel and Rosewood have the guard outside activate the alarm, causing Karla and company to end their crime a tad early.

The armored truck they're driving nearly runs over Axel as it escapes. Rosewood gets his hands on a cement mixer, picks Axel up and starts a pursuit.

Taggart, meanwhile, tries to flag down a car he can commandeer.

The chase continues with the cement truck accidentally smashing into other cars and causing all kinds of damage. This is much as the mack truck did at the beginning of the first film, right down to squad cars in pursuit that get involved in a variety of accidents.

Eventually they find the truck, abandoned. Nearby, however, lie the tracks of a pickup vehicle. The duo, soon joined by Taggart in an unmarked police car, trace it to the Playboy mansion.

Once again Axel cons his way in. He pretends to be a pool cleaner assigned to remove human excretion from the pool. Taggart and Rosewood pass as supervisors. If nothing else, this scene gets another song on the soundtrack and offers the audience lots of shots of scantily clad Playboy bunnies.

Axel catches sight of Dent, Karla and Thomopolous and creates a bit of a scene. This results in Hugh Hefner throwing them all out of the party.

Back in the car, the film reveals that Axel picked Dent's wallet and now has the name of his accountant, Sidney Bernstein.

At the precinct, Lutz, Mayor Egan and the three cops meet about the crimes, with Lutz screaming at everybody. The mayor is obviously growing tired of the man's verbal abuse.

Later, they go to see Bernstein, who was clearly designed to serve as this film's Bronson Pinchot, and tell him that he's under arrest for twenty five unpaid parking tickets. Bernstein subtly offers a bribe, which Axel accepts. He then says he will have to use Bernstein's computer to erase the tickets from the police department computer. Bernstein happily leaves his office.

While in the office, Axel calls Jan and learns that Dent's holdings include a race track, a gun club and oil refineries. Apparently, the man is having financial problems. The insurance on all his properties has lapsed, except for that on the race track.

This leads the team there to the expected site of the "E" crime. Dent plans to have his own track robbed for the insurance money.

The robbery takes place on schedule, and Tony Scott cuts the cameras between Karla and company in action and the horses running their race.

Karla picks up a gun and turns it on Cain for all of his screw-ups. She pulls the trigger, killing him instantly. Afterward, Karla, dressed in black, sits next to Dent and kisses him.

BEVERLY HILLS COP II

The police arrive on the premises, and Lutz claims the alphabet bandit, Chip Cain, has been killed by the race track's security guard.

Axel catches sight of oil washed from a horse which had been grazing in Dent's oil field.

They arrive and see a series of trucks and cars parked near the refineries. Axel recognizes the dirt as matching that found on Bogomil's shoes.

They investigate one of the trucks and find it filled with weapons. This delights Billy.

Rosewood, trying to imitate what Axel had done earlier, accidentally triggers an alarm, alerting Dent and his people to their presence.

This turns into a giant shootout as Rosewood uses a rocket launcher to blow up one of the escaping munition trucks. The guns continue firing.

Amazingly, Rosewood and Taggart convince twenty armed men to surrender to them, just as backup squad cars arrive.

Axel comes face to face with Dent, but a henchman tries to shoot him. This allows Dent the opportunity to escape.

Moments later, he drives a car through the wall and Foley squeezes the trigger of his gun. The bullet find its mark in the center of Dent's head and the car crashes through another wall and explodes.

Axel, knocked aside, tries to regain his feet, when he sees Karla standing over him about to shoot her gun. At the last moment, she is shot down by Taggart.

Lutz arrives with the mayor, furious at the scene he witnesses. Rosewood points out that they solved the alphabet crimes, which were all part of a mass weapons deal.

Feeling they went over his head, Lutz fires Taggart and Rosewood, but is fired himself by Mayor Egan, who thanks Axel for all his help.

A happy ending, with the recovering Bogomil promoted to chief of police and Mayor Egan calling Inspector Todd to commend Axel. Todd tells Axel to get his butt home, adding that Jeffrey has had an accident with the Ferrari.

In the next scene, Axel bids farewell to Taggart and Rosewood and speeds off on his way.

The strength of *Beverly Hills Cop II* lies in the developing relationship between Axel, Taggart, Rosewood and Bogomil. Their friendship has deepened since the first film. Good performances by Brigitte Neilson as Karla and Jurgen Prochnow, who would make a great James Bond villain, as Dent add to the production.

Director Tony Scott tries to keep things moving at a steady clip, much as he did with *Top Gun*. Unfortunately, there's only so much he can do with the Larry Ferguson/Warren Skarren screenplay. The story is full of holes. Nothing seems fresh. This is the worst kind of sequel; one that strives for nothing more than repetition. Despite all this, the film grossed $150 million in the United States alone.

If there is a *Beverly Hills Cop III,* and the rumors *are* growing stronger, one can only hope the film-makers will show more respect for their audience and themselves.

EDDIE MURPHY faces the camera flanked by producers Don Simpson (left) and Jerry Bruckheimer (right) during the filming of BEVERLY HILLS COP II....

"MURPHY'S MOST HILARIOUS PERFORMANCE."
— Peter Travers, PEOPLE MAGAZINE

"EDDIE, THE CROWN PRINCE OF COMEDY…
KING SIZE LAUGHS. YOU'LL HAVE A
ROYAL GOOD TIME." — Pat Collins, WWOR-TV

"HE'S MORE THAN A GREAT
COMIC. HE'S A WONDERFUL
ACTOR… POSITIVELY REGAL
AS THE PRINCE…" — Joel Siegel,
GOOD MORNING AMERICA

"A ROYAL FLUSH…
EDDIE'S THE REIGNING
KING OF COMEDY…"
— Kathleen Carroll, NEW YORK DAILY NEWS

"THE FUNNIEST
EDDIE MURPHY
PICTURE YET."
— Ben Yagoda,
PHILADELPHIA DAILY NEWS

EDDIE MURPHY

COMING TO
AMERICA

PARAMOUNT PICTURES PRESENTS
AN EDDIE MURPHY PRODUCTION
A LANDIS/FOLSEY FILM EDDIE MURPHY · COMING TO AMERICA
ARSENIO HALL · JAMES EARL JONES · JOHN AMOS
MADGE SINCLAIR · SHARI HEADLEY
Executive Producers LESLIE BELZBERG and MARK LIPSKY
Story by EDDIE MURPHY
Screenplay by DAVID SHEFFIELD & BARRY W. BLAUSTEIN
Produced by ROBERT D. WACHS and GEORGE FOLSEY, JR.
Directed by JOHN LANDIS DOLBY STEREO
IN SELECTED THEATRES
Original Soundtrack Album Available on   A PARAMOUNT PICTURE
ATCO Records, Cassettes and Compact Discs

□ Coming to America....

"While Murphy's new film—part farce, part old-fashioned romance—is hardly ground breaking. Murphy's performance is....He acts with a beguiling simplicity that lifts the movie into the top ranks of hot-weather entertainment. Swaggering, swearing and scene-hogging are out this time. Murphy shares the jokes with real-life pal Arsenio Hall....Expect no surprise at [the film's] outcome. Delight instead in Murphy's easy banter with Hall. And keep an eye out for the two in various cameo roles, cleverly disguised by makeup whiz Rick Baker.....This is Murphy's most heartfelt and hilarious performance. And his riskiest. Audiences may miss the foul-mouthed wiseguy they took to their hearts. Will they accept the mature Murphy, who plans to take on his first dramatic role in the film of the Pulitzer prizewinning play *Fences*? Let's hope so. *Coming to America* shows Eddie Murphy's talent has only begun to be tapped."

—People

"The most surprising thing about Eddie Murphy's *Coming to America* is its sweetness, its mildness, its old fashioned one-step-at-a-time pace. For those who felt battered by *Beverly Hills Cop II* and ripped off by *The Golden Child*, this will come as a relief. For those who loved those movies, this is bound to seem a letdown.....*Coming to America* may be more interesting as a career move than a movie. Murphy is repositioning himself as a star: gone is the smirk, the trademark barking laugh. As Akeem, he stays totally in character, with a sweet African lilt in his voice. It's a likable, restrained star turn, but he's at his funniest when he pops up, heavily disguised, in three other cameo roles.....In these wonderful characters, a kind of affectionate survey of the urban black scene, *Coming to America* sparks to life. Inside this elaborately produced romantic comedy there's a little Spike Lee movie struggling to get out.....You've got to admire producer Murphy for his commitment to black actors: there's never been a black romantic comedy on this scale before, and what freshness it has comes from such scenes as the uproarious Black Awareness pageant where Akeem first spots his beloved....."

—Newsweek

THE CRITICS

By the time *Beverly Hills Cop II* appeared in theaters, Eddie Murphy felt he had played the wise-cracking cop enough. He wanted a more challenging role. Swearing to avoid a purely dramatic characterization, he desperately wanted to play someone more comfortable with words than with guns.

The role of Prince Akeem in *Coming to America* fit his plan perfectly.

The opening sequences of *Coming to America* effectively portray how tedious being a member of a royal family can be. Absolutely everything, from brushing his teeth to wiping his heine, is done for Prince Akeem of Zamunda. He hates his life, particularly his arranged marriage to a woman he's never met. He wants someone to love him for himself, not because she has been told to.

His parents, the King and Queen, assure him that he will eventually learn to love her. Akeem doesn't think so and eventually convinces his father to let him go to America. The King thinks he's going to satisfy his sexual yearnings, but the Prince is intent on finding a woman to fall in love with.

The King grants him 40 days of life in America.

Along with his assistant and best friend, Semmi, he travels to the place in America he hopes will be perfect for finding a bride for a Prince, Queens.

They ultimately end up in one of the worst neighborhoods imaginable. This excites Akeem as they will seem like ordinary African students on a visit to America. They wander into a local barber shop where a group of customers argue about nothing. This is a significant scene, as the magic make-up of Rick Baker converts both Eddie Murphy and Arsenio Hall into various characters. You haven't seen movie make-up, until you've seen Eddie Murphy as an elderly white Jewish man!

The duo move into a rat-infested building. Semmi is repulsed at the living arrangements, while Akeem, the eternal optimist, thinks they're great, even after all their luggage is stolen.

Akeem suggests they buy clothes which will make them look like common New Yorkers, and that's what they do. It's significant to note that as Akeem, Murphy has moved far from his previous characterizations. Akeem's gentleness and innocence is a refreshing change of pace from the motor-mouth dialogue of Axel Foley. Mur-

phy proves he possesses greater range than previously demonstrated.

The search begins as Akeem and Semmi start hitting the club scene, encountering one weird woman after another. Each exhibits incredible peculiarities.

They encounter then the barber they'd met earlier and are told that the Black Awareness Rally would be the perfect place to meet a nice woman.

The Africans attend and Akeem finally catches sight of Lisa McDowall. Lisa addresses the crowd, requesting that everyone contribute to the building of a new park.

Baskets are handed around for donations and Lisa's actor boyfriend Darryl, who works for SoulGlo hair products, contributes nothing. Akeem, on the other hand, contributes a wad of bills.

The emcee of the event delivers a plug for Lisa's father's restaurant, McDowalls, telling where the store is located. Akeem makes a mental note of the address.

The next day, he and Semmi get jobs there as janitors. Cleo McDowall shows them how to clean windows. While Cleo does so, a photographer from McDonalds snaps photos of the storefront, which infuriates him.

It seems a constant legal battle rages between the two restaurants, with the Golden Arches attempting to drive the Golden Arc out of business.

It really is quite humorous to watch John Amos portray Cleo desperately pointing out the differences between the two restaurants.

Akeem, now dressed in a McDowall's uniform, cleans and introduces himself to Lisa. She's busy doing the accounting.

From the conversation, it's obvious Akeem is an innocent, a trait which amuses Lisa in a nice way.

Darryl enters the restaurant, gives Cleo a pair of Jets tickets and then takes Lisa out on a date. Before departing, he asks Akeem to dispose of his strawberry shake and throws it at him, the cup's contents splattering on his shirt. Semmi thinks this hysterical, until a look from Akeem silences him.

Later, Akeem goes back to the barber shop, certainly a strange place to seek the wisdom of the world. He is told by various patrons that he should get in tight with the girl's father. This in turn will put him close to the woman he desires.

Considering this advice, he returns to work and attempts to start a conversation with Cleo, but it doesn't work out. One of the workers points to Lisa and Darryl, noting that there's no way he could compete with a guy who can offer her any material thing her heart desires. In response, he anonymously mails her a $500,000 pair of earrings.

Lisa and her sister Patrice come to the restaurant. In a moment's time Akeem is invited to the basketball game Darryl has tickets for, but as Patrice's date. At the game, Darryl constantly makes snide remarks regarding Akeem's coming from Africa, while Patrice squeezes his leg and comes on to him. Excusing himself, he goes to the men's room. While on line, one of the vendors, a former citizen of Zamunda, praises him, but Akeem tries to dissuade him from doing so.

The next day at the restaurant, Darryl tries to get Lisa to quit her job. She doesn't want to.

He goes to get her coffee, and a moment later Lisa asks Akeem to sit and talk to her for a minute. She says he seems different, nicely different, from the other people working there.

Their conversation is interrupted by a shotgun-toting robber who tries rob the cash register. Akeem, utilizing his mop handle, approaches the man and asks him to lower his weapon. The man refuses, and Akeem uses the handle as a bow-staff to sweep the man's legs out from under him. The shotgun goes flying and Semmi grabs it and aims it at the robber just as he starts to get up with a switchblade in his hand. Seeing no choice, the man lowers the blade.

The action in this scene is not exactly what an audience expects from Akeem. Axel Foley or Reggie Hammond might act this way, but not this peaceful African prince. It's an exciting moment, and one that impresses Lisa.

In contrast, Darryl cowered in the corner. Later, Cleo thanks the men and asks them to come to his home that Saturday night. Akeem thinks this is wonderful until he learns he only wants them to serve as bartenders and valets, parking cars.

At the party, Darryl talks to Cleo. Moments later, Darryl announces that he and Lisa are going to be engaged. This is news to her and the announcement provokes nothing but anger. She pulls him into another room and vents her anger. She then steps into the backyard.

Akeem joins her, placing his jacket over her shoulders. She tells him that she will not be pressured into marriage, a sentiment Akeem certainly shares. They talk and it soon becomes obvious a spark has been ignited between them.

The next day, Semmi is in a particularly foul mood, sick of living like a peasant. Akeem tells him *he* is going to work, and that things are going well with Lisa.

After work, he and Lisa get together and agree to have dinner at Akeem's home. He then refuses to let her in when he peeks inside and finds that Semmi has totally redone the apartment. It now possesses every luxury, down to a hot tub in the middle of the room.

Akeem takes his "pocket money," a wad of bills big enough to choke a horse, and joins Lisa in the hall. They agree to go out to dinner. She thinks he's embarrassed by his home.

They walk through the park and find two winos sleeping by a park bench. He takes the money out of his pocket and gives it to them, telling Lisa, who hasn't seen the amount, that it's just pocket change.

The two walk off, and the winos, in an inspired bit of in-joking, sit up. They turn out to be Randolph and Mortimer Duke from *Trading Places*. They were made penniless by Murphy and Dan Aykroyd in that film. Randolph's reaction to the money is to say, "Mortimer, we're back!" Mortimer's response is to just smile. Then the pair pass the restaurant the couple dines in, and thank him through the window.

As the night continues, it becomes very obvious Lisa has fallen for him.

Meanwhile, Semmi sends a telegram to the King, requesting $500,000 in additional funds. He says he and Akeem have run low at cash.

Returning home, he finds Patrice, who has been waiting for Akeem and doesn't understand how they own so many things their small salary.

Outside, Akeem sings in the streets. When he comes home, he's shocked to find Patrice in bed with Semmi, who has passed himself off as a prince. She promises to keep it a secret.

The next day, Lisa tells her father she's going to the museum with Akeem. He isn't pleased at all but would rather she stay with Darryl. At least he's rich.

She departs for her date, thrilling Akeem beyond words.

Things go downhill quickly when the King and Queen, alarmed by Semmi's telegram, arrive in New York seeking out Akeem. They are alarmed that he has been living as a peasant and begin searching for him, first at McDowall's restaurant and then at the man's home.

Cleo quickly learns that Akeem is actually rich, and then tries to play matchmaker, despite the King's claim that his son came to America to sew his wild oats.

Lisa learns the truth and is furious at Akeem for making her fall in love with a lie. He pleads for understanding, but it seems she's closed him out of her life.

Naturally things eventually work out as Lisa coming to grips with her true feelings for Akeem. She finally understands why he pretended to be poor.

By film's end, they are married in Zamunda and, as in all fairy tales, cliched though it may be, they live happily ever after.

Everyone involved with *Coming to America* should be proud of themselves. They deliver a wonderful film that comes across as very old-fashioned in a pleasant sort of way.

Eddie Murphy has never been more sensitive or touching in a portrayal. His Akeem is a believable romantic figure. Arsenio Hall brings just the right element of exasperation as Semmi, a man born to the trappings of wealth but reduced to poverty by his Prince. James Earl Jones as the King is as splendid as he always is, while Madge Sinclair brings just the right amount of class to her role as the Queen. John Amos is in fine form as a supporting character, and newcomer Shari Headley makes Lisa a real human being, torn by emotion but eventually giving in to her heart.

Credit should also be given to director John Landis, who has put his often juvenile attempts at humor aside to deliver a first rate romantic comedy that may eventually be considered a classic of the genre. A special nod is due Eddie Murphy as one of the few black actors in Hollywood with the power to cast a film with black actors and have it score successfully with the mainstream audience.

EDDIE MURPHY RICHARD PRYOR

They're up to something big.

HARLEM NIGHTS

PARAMOUNT PICTURES PRESENTS IN ASSOCIATION WITH EDDIE MURPHY PRODUCTIONS A FILM BY EDDIE MURPHY
EDDIE MURPHY RICHARD PRYOR

HARLEM NIGHTS MUSIC BY HERBIE HANCOCK DIRECTOR OF PHOTOGRAPHY WOODY OMENS, A.S.C. EDITED BY GEORGE BOWERS PRODUCTION DESIGN BY LAWRENCE G. PAULL EXECUTIVE PRODUCER EDDIE MURPHY
PRODUCED BY ROBERT D. WACHS AND MARK LIPSKY WRITTEN AND DIRECTED BY EDDIE MURPHY A PARAMOUNT PICTURE

□ Harlem Nights....

"Judged strictly as entertainment, *Harlem Nights* is, at best, marginally diverting.....It's a poorly paced, unimaginatively written genre piece that has absolutely no feel for its era or its locale. With its nightclub settings, you might hope for some great music and spectacle, but this doesn't seem to interest Murphy, who as the film's executive producer, writer, director and star can take full responsibility for the movie's listless tone, as well as his own oddly disengaged performance. Murphy's notion of comedy can best be described as infantile; his idea of wit is frequently repeated four-letter words. Much more intriguing is *Harlem Night"* vengeful subtext. What are we to make of the role Murphy has written for himself, and in which we are supposed to find him as endearingly irrepressible as ever? We first meet Quick as a little boy, when he shoots a man point blank in the head. Before the movie is over the lovable Murphy gets to (1) slug an elderly woman in the stomach and shoot off her toe; (2) shoot a gangster's moll through the head after sleeping with her; (3) murder three pursuers; (4) blow up a roomful of gangsters. It's nice the world's most popular screen comic wants to share his colorful fantasy life with us, but perhaps he should have saved it for his shrink."

—**Newsweek**

"Making his directing debut....Murphy has created a facsimile of 1930s Harlem on a Hollywood back lot. He has brought together three generations of black comedians. And, with his script, he may have set a big-screen record for most frequent use of the big, bad, 12-letter expletive suggesting maternal incest. *Harlem Nights*, after all, is about being *bad* (meaning good). The movie, however, is just bad (meaning bad)......After making seven movies that have grossed a total of $1 billion worldwide, Murphy is Hollywood's King Midas. His movies make money even when they are indisputably bad. As he himself admitted to *Rolling Stone*, *Beverly Hills Cop II* (1987), which grossed $275 million, was a 'half-assed movie—probably the most successful mediocre picture in history.' He also said that *The Golden Child* (1986), which made more than $115 million, was 'a piece of shit.' By those standards, *Harlem Nights* is Hollywood gold."

—**New York**

THE CRITICS

117

In the eight years since his motion picture debut, Eddie Murphy had continued to amass tremendous power in Hollywood. He went starring in films to co-producing them and supplying initial storylines. In the case of *Harlem Nights,* he took on the additional duties of screenwriter and director.

The film opens in Harlem in 1918. The young Quick makes a delivery to the gambling room of Sugar Ray's speak-easy, where a variety of men are playing poker.

When Quick walks in, one man begins bitching that kids bring him bad luck, but no one will listen. He rolls the dice and craps out. Furious, he whips out a blade and sticks it under Sugar Ray's chin, demanding not only the money he lost, but all the money Ray brought in that night.

Sugar Ray tries to calm the man, while frantically reaching under the table for his gun that's supposed to be there. Unfortunately, it's not!

The man is about to stab him when a gunshot is heard. The bullet finds its target in the center of the man's forehead. Quick had grabbed the hidden gun and killed the man that was going to hurt them. Everyone in the room is shocked.

The film is a bit startling for the audience as well.

Ray, regaining his composure, offers to take Quick home. He learns that the boy is an orphan. Considering this, he tells the youth he can stay with him for a few days, and the boy accepts.

This opening sequence foreshadows the film. One disconcerting fact, however, is that the infamous "f" word is used fifteen times in a matter of about 90 seconds.

The film flashes forward 20 years and Ray's Place has become Club Sugar-Ray. Quick has grown up to be Eddie Murphy!

Immediately the audience is made aware that Sugar Ray has had a great deal of success with his gambling/prostitution business. He and Quick are sitting at a table overseeing the action when Tommy Smalls comes in with Dominique LaRue, mistress of gangster Bugsy Calhoune. Quick is obviously taken by her, but Sugar Ray warns him to keep his distance.

Quick nonetheless introduces himself, while Ray is called over to one of the gaming tables where the near-sighted Bennie refuses to wear his glasses and is making all the wrong calls.

It's a pretty funny moment when Ray pulls the man aside and requests that he put on his glasses. Bennie does so, even though he thinks he doesn't need them.

Elsewhere, Bugsy Calhoune grows angry that Tommy Smalls, an employee, has been ripping him off. Tony insists that Smalls wouldn't rip anyone off, convinced because he had hand-picked the man.

Bugsy acknowledges that, in a sense, it's Tony's fault. He then questions him about Club Sugar Ray.

Feeling the club is hurting business, Bugsy suggests Sugar Ray be visited by Phil Cantone, and shut down.

Before Tony goes, Bugsy teaches him a lesson about hiring the wrong people. He places his hand under the top of a piano, then allows it to fall and break his fingers. He then tells him to use his good hand to slit Tommy Small's throat from one side to the other.

At Club Sugar Ray, Ray is going over the night's receipts. Quick has Vera, the club's Madam, come in, because he thinks somebody's holding back. The money from the girls just doesn't jive with the amount of business the club did that night.

Vera takes offense, and calls Quick into the back alley to settle the matter. Quick goes out back, laughing hysterically at the idea of them fighting until Vera delivers a powerful punch to his face, followed quickly by a second blow.

He retaliates by delivering a punch to her gut, which doubles her over, but only for a second. She rises and Quick starts delivering a series of punches.

She ultimately beats him up and it ends with Quick knocking her down with a garbage can. Vera then gets back up, pulling out a razor. Quick whips out his pistol and warns her back. When she refuses, he shoots off her pinkie toe. That brings the fight to an end.

These sequences are mean-spirited, but there's no denying that the fight sequence works wonderfully. It's a shock to see Della Reese beat the crap out of Eddie Murphy, but it's hysterical to watch Quick go from laughing off the situation to shooting off the woman's toe out of anger.

Sugar Ray comes home to find Sergeant Phil Cantone in his living room. Cantone, acting as politely as he can, while subtly inferring that a black man shouldn't live the way Ray does, questions him about the club. Ray says he's got the wrong man as he has run a candy store for the past twenty years.

Cantone acts as though he accepts this and leaves. The audience, and Ray, know better.

At dinner, Ray talks about relocating to avoid trouble with Bugsy, but Quick hates the idea. He believes they should fight the mobster rather than run. Ray feels Bugsy is too powerful to oppose.

The local boxing champ comes to their table at that moment, chats for a few minutes and then wanders off. Quick discusses how they're going to make a killing handling the bets for the fight. The champ's opponent, a white man, will have 3-1 odds placed on him and every white person betting on the fight will undoubtedly bet on him.

The next day, Quick gets a letter from Dominique, requesting that he meet her for dinner. Ray suggests he not go see her, but Quick wants to know whether she's still with Calhoune.

Before Quick can leave, Ray catches sight of Phil Cantone. He has come to the club and is "surprised" to find that Ray is the Sugar Ray he was looking for. Cantone wants to talk business, so they go the office where he lays out the deal: Calhoune wants ten of their fifteen thousand dollars take each week. Ray asks if he can get back to him, but Cantone says he'll get back to them.

A meeting is called at Ray's house an hour later. While they concede that they're going to have to close shop, the develop a scheme to make $50,000 each by ripping off Bugsy Calhoune's bookies who will be handling the big fight. In fact, they're going to bet on the white fighter, which will increase the payoff, and talk the champ into taking a dive.

When everyone else leaves, Ray suggests that Quick talk to Tommy Smalls and

In HARLEM NIGHTS, Eddie Murphy is the adopted son of Richard Pryor, owner of Club Sugar Ray....

find out whatever he can about Cantone.

Danny Aiello as Sergeant Phil Cantone in a pleasant turnabout from the actor's usual roles. The actor usually plays loving, compassionate characters, but is tremendous at portraying low-key villainy. Although his Cantone always smiles, every one of his words is set with a condescending undertone. The audience gains a sense that he truly resents the idea of a black man having money, while he, as is pointed out, is living in a "hubble!"

The film cuts to Tommy Smalls' apartment building as he's about to step out of the elevator. Cantone is waiting for him and delivers a punch directly to his face. Tommy's date flees. When the man awakens in his apartment, Cantone and Tony are standing there, voicing Calhoune's complaint that he had stolen $5,000. Tommy proclaims his innocence, but his words fall on deaf ears. Cantone pulls his gun and empties it into him. Tony then proceeds to cut his throat.

Cantone then meets with Calhoune, tells him about Tommy and adds that the people from Club Sugar Ray have bet $200,000 on the white fighter. Assuming the champ will be throwing the fight, Calhoune tells Cantone to put $500,000 on the 3-1 underdog to win. Meanwhile, Quick shows up at Tommy Smalls' apartment and finds his corpse. Shocked, he leaves the building and drives off, only to be seen by Tommy's brother, Crying Man.

That is how he's billed on the credits.

After leaving, Quick meets Dominique for dinner. He is surprised to find Calhoune sitting at their table.

Calhoune asks Quick to work for his organization, but is summarily dismissed. Quick leaves and Calhoune turns to Dominique, asking if the man is someone she could...ah, make love to. She replies in the affirmative.

Quick leaves the restaurant, and Crying Man tells his boys to kill him. An exciting and humorous car chase follows in which Arsenio continues to cry over his brother's death, and then, when crashing into Quick's car, accidentally shoots one of his own people. The sequence ends quite humorously as Quick squeezes off three shots at his machine gun-wielding opponents, killing each of them. Suffice to say, the se-

Richard Pryor and EDDIE MURPHY in front of
Club Sugar Ray....

quence, a truly funny one, plays far more humorously than it can be described. Arsenio Hall, who had done so well in his previous team-up with Murphy, *Coming to America*, brings much needed comic relief to the film. He provides just the right moment of zaniness.

Returning to Club Sugar Ray, Quick tells everyone about his evening. Ray gets a phone call detailing who Calhoune's bag man is for the fight, and he gets Vera to find the right woman to get through to the man. Then a phone call comes from Dominique. She asks Quick to come to her house to spend some time alone. Once there, they chat for a few minutes and then proceed to the bedroom. Dominique goes into the bathroom. At that moment Quick finds a little pistol, which he kisses and thinks cute, placed under her pillow, noting that he thought he was the only person ever to sleep that way. His amusement passes, as contemplates the reason for the gun.

Moments later, Dominique comes out of the bathroom and gets into bed with him. The two proceed to make love. Hours later, they talk as Domnique reaches under the pillow, pulls out the gun and notes, "Sorry, Quick, it's only business."

She clicks the trigger on and empty chamber.

"This is personal!" he responds as he whips out his own gun and blows her away.

Quick's ruthlessness in this scene is startling, but one has to keep in mind that this woman was about to kill him. His actions are justified. As Dominique, Jasmine Guy delivers an impressive characterization, easily dismissing the image of her as Whitley from television's *A Different World*. She is sexy, vulnerable and cold-hearted all at the same time. This is an auspicious motion picture debut.

At a local bar, Vera's woman meets with Richie Vento, Calhoune's bag-man. She begins to seduce him. An easy victim, he really falls for her as time goes on. In fact, after they've made love, he calls his wife and tells her he's not coming home anymore.

Quick goes to see Sugar Ray, telling him absolutely everything that's happened.

Quick wants blood, but Ray convinces him to play it cool until their scam goes down.

Later, Cantone shows up and arrests everybody, shutting the club down. He doesn't arrest Ray, wanting him to turn over Quick. He then leaves.

Sugar Ray departs shortly later and finds Calhoune's car waiting for him. He gets in and has a conversation with the gangster. He's told that Calhoune wants him and Quick to move elsewhere.

After this little meeting, Ray goes down to the police station and bails out all of his patrons.

The next day at Bennie's apartment, there's a really schmaltzy scene in which Quick apologizes to Vera for shooting her toe off, and she expresses her motherly love. This sequence of the film does not work. It appears only to tie up loose ends.

Later, after Calhoune has announced that he wants Club Sugar Ray closed down permanently, Ray shows up to look at the charred remains of his establishment. The fire may not have been shown as a budget-saving measure. That night, as the big fight takes place, two of Ray's men clear the crowd from one of Calhoune's clubs. They set off a bomb that destroys the place.

The film then cuts to an alley where the collected money from Calhoune's bookies is loaded into Richie's car. He drives off, unexpectedly followed by Cantone.

Richie picks up his new girlfriend, Vera's woman, who is carrying a laundry sack. This is thrown into the trunk, right next to an identical sack containing the money.

Ray's people arrange a traffic accident that holds Richie at bay while Ray and Quick, dressed as cops, pull up and tell him the accident is the least of his problems. They say the woman he's with is known as Lady Heroin, and she's going down. They reach into the trunk for the supposed forty pounds of drugs, but take the sack of money.

Cantone watches and smiles. Another squad car pulls up and the two white cops within talk to Richie in private. He reveals he's on a run for Calhoune. They tell the other cops, Ray and Quick to let the man go about his business and take the sack of money.

Meanwhile, the white fighter loses and Calhoune realizes he's been set up.

Quick and Ray go to a bank that's been closed for five years and are followed by Cantone. He pulls his gun on them and talks about their con, which worked pretty well until a couple of real cops showed up.

Quick tells Cantone that they're making a deposit, at which point a group of Ray's men level shotguns at him. Cantone is tied up and left in the vault. He is told to take tiny breaths to conserve air, and that someone will be back to get him on Monday morning.

Richie arrives at Bugsy's place, empties the bag and realizes the cops took the wrong bag. He tells Bugsy everything, and the gangster is furious that a million dollars of his money was given to a pair of cops for numerous bags of sugar, not heroin.

Bugsy makes the connection and is furious. Vera suddenly shows up, claiming no participation in the rip-off and tells him Ray and Quick are at Ray's house.

Calhoune, pretending to be concerned over her welfare, gives her his phone number should she have any problems. Bugsy and his men show up at Ray's and find no one there. They do, however, find Cantone's hat and badge.

Bugsy tries to figure out what's going on and suddenly realizes it's a set-up. Just then, the front door opens, triggering an explosion that kills them all.

Elsewhere, the cops from the accident shake the hands of Ray and Quick as they were part of the sting and have been paid equal shares. Ray and Quick say they've got a tank of gas and a trunk filled with money, so they might as well get started on their journey.

Harlem Nights is an enjoyable movie, despite much of it being derivative of Paul Newman and Robert Redford's *The Sting*. The biggest problem with the film is that although the production design conveys the era the story is depicting, little else does. Everyone speaks much as they do today, which is highly incongruous with the 30's setting.

The cast is tremendous, from Redd Foxx as Bennie and Della Reese as Vera, the old team from TV's *Sanford and Son*, to Danny Aiello as Cantone and Richard Pryor as Sugar Ray. The only stereotypical character is Bugsy Calhoune, adequately played

126

EDDIE MURPHY makes sweet love to Dominique La Rue, but the deadly mobster mistress has other things in mind....

by Michael Lerner. He does what he can with the material.

While he still has some distance to grow as a film-maker, Eddie Murphy delivers an impressive job as writer and director. He is comfortable giving equal time to his other performers, not worrying about his own screen time. In fact, there are many aspects of Quick which make him unlikable, a first for a Murphy characterization.

Murphy certainly deserves another crack at directing, and did not warrant the critical roasting he received.

Another 48 Hours....

This analysis is based on an early draft of the film's screenplay, dated October 30, 1989. It is assumed to be quite similar to the final shooting script.

A group of bikers meet at a cantina in Death Valley and discuss working for someone known as Iceman. One biker, Malcolm Price, is being paid a great deal of money to assassinate Reggie Hammond. Upon being told of his target's identity, Price admits he almost killed Hammond in prison, only he was being protected by "the brothers". They also mention there's been a pricetag on Hammond's head for the past five years.

Money and various weapons are exchanged until they're interrupted by a cop with warrants for their arrest stemming for stealing a car. One of the men, Hickok, raises his weapon and blows the cop through the window. Another, Brother Ed, shoots the tires of the squad car, trapping the cop's partner, who is also killed.

During the mayhem, the bartender tries calling the police and is shot for his trouble.

The audience learns that Hammond is scheduled to be released from prison the following week. The bikers take off as the film cuts to Folsom prison.

Hammond is before the warden, having sliced open a man's stomach for trying to rape him. Reggie explains that there's a price on his head because he had stolen money from someone named Iceman who also wants him dead because he knows his face. The warden refuses to believe this, and states that he is going to recommend Hammond's sentence be extended one more time.

Hammond explains that he and his lawyer will go public with the many inconsistencies of prison policy which allows inmates to shoot drugs and get laid. The warden considers this for a moment.

"Given all the trouble you've been having," he notes, "maybe it would be best if you spent your remaining three days in isolation."

EDDIE MURPHY and Nick Nolte are back together again for ANOTHER 48 HOURSE....

At the Bay Meadows Racetrack, Detective Jack Cates stakes out two men he believes to be working for Iceman, who he happens to be investigating. He follows them into a barn and overhears them talking about a "hit". One of the men is back-up for the bikers in case they miss their target. The proposed assassin says he will accept the assignment, and money is loaded into his nylon bag. A photo of Reggie Hammond is handed to him as well, but before he can react, Cates steps out of the shadows, gun in hand.

An exciting shoot-out follows, resulting in one of the men being killed and the assassin escaping. Cates reaches into the bag and finds the photo of Hammond, which he shoves into his pocket.

Shortly later, the police swarm over the sight of the shooting. Fellow officer Ben Kehoe approaches Cates, telling him there was nothing wrong with the victim as the man most definitely was an employee of the racetrack. Cates can't understand it. He was on a stakeout for the Iceman case and saw an exchange, thus gaining probably cause to act.

Blake Wilson from Internal Affairs doesn't see it quite the same way. It's apparent they've run into each other before, and equally obvious there is no love lost between them. Wilson doesn't believe there is an Iceman. He believes the detectives have spent the past five years pursuing an imaginary criminal. The way he sees it, Cates shot an innocent man, a theory reinforced by Kehoe and the other detectives being unable to find the murdered man's supposed weapon.

Wilson asks a woman detective named Creal about bullets, and her response is that there are two in the body and one in the wall, all apparently from Cates' gun. Wilson gives the order that the place be stripped bare if that's what it takes to find a gun. "And if there wasn't," he says to Cates, "I don't think the Iceman's going to save your ass."

The film cuts to a court room on a later date as Cates is indicted for manslaughter. Bail is set at $350,000. All of the detectives in attendance are shocked, and Wilson approaches Jack to tell him the review board will be meeting in two days.

Cates' lawyer points out that Jack is being made an example, but he believes he can get the judge to grant a few hours to get the money together.

Kehoe says that whatever he's got is Jack's, but Cates states that he'll take care of it himself.

In Folsom prison, Reggie Hammond plays basketball by himself, surrounded by armed guards. Cates approaches and Hammond reveals his anger at Jack for not coming to see him over the past five years. He says he thought they were friends.

Cates replies he was busy, adding that he's taking Reggie's money. Anger swells and Hammond punches Cates in the face, sending the guards swarming all over him.

Explaining that he thought Hammond should know, Cates turns around to leave. Hammond is not happy.

Two days later, Hammond gets ready to leave Folsom. Tyrone Robinson, described as "a 50 year old Mean Joe Green—Grisled, but still powerful," approaches him. Robinson warns Hammond that he had better get his money, because he kept him alive in prison. He says he will, and then approaches the warden, who gives him the standard "gift" for released convicts: 50 dollars and a bus ride to San Francisco.

Hammond steps through the front gate and sees the awaiting bus, as well as Cates leaning against his Cadillac convertible. Cates tries to explain that he's in trouble, and that he's after the Iceman, a person he believes is after Hammond. He produces the photo he'd picked up earlier and hands it to Reggie. He's got 48 hours to get his hands on the criminal or he himself is going to go to jail.

Hammond either has nothing to offer or refuses to impart the information. Left with no choice, Cates rides off and Hammond boards the bus.

Cates stops at a nearby diner. Hammond's bus, meanwhile, is moving down the road. A motorcycle and another vehicle fall in behind it. Sitting at the diner's counter, Cates looks outside just in time to see the bus roar by closely followed by the two vehicles.

The car cuts in front of the bus and slows down, forcing the bus to do the same. Hammond glances out a window and sees the motorcycle riding Cherry, and there is a flicker of recognition. Cherry pulls a sawed off shotgun out of a shoulder bag and fires at Hammond. Reggie ducks as the window shatters.

An exciting "hunt" follows as the killers fire at the bus. The bus finally slides down the road on its side, forcing a tractor tailer carrying telephone poles to swerve.

The truck still gets struck by the bus, and its cargo unspools.

Later, Hammond and the other passengers are treated for their injuries. Cates approaches Hammond, and offers him a ride in his Caddy.

Meanwhile, Burroughs is in his hotel room, watching a news report about the accident. He learns there were only two injuries and no fatalities. He shuts off the TV and goes back to the work at hand, wiring a bomb.

While driving, Cates explains his situation to Hammond, adding that if they find the Iceman, Reggie will get his money back. If they don't, the odds are good that Hammond will be killed.

Hammond points out that he shouldn't be surprised by the events, as he's been screwed over innumerable times during the past five years.

Cates reveals that he knows there was a payroll robbery and that the money was found in Hammond's cell, so there was certainly question as to his innocence.

Hammond says he was set up, which to Cates is an old story, until Reggie points out that the cops still haven't found the gun of Cates' victim and asks if that make him guilty.

Cates admits he has a good point.

In the same conversation, humor is derived from Hammond making fun of Cates' car, which turns out to be the same model, year and color as the one he drove in the first film. The film also conveys that he and girlfriend Elaine were married shortly after the conclusion of the events in the first film, but that a year later she left him because he wasn't sensitive to her needs.

The duo arrive at Cates' house, which is currently up for sale. Reggie's Porsche Speedster is in the driveway. The way Cates looks at it, part of the house is Reggie's, because he "borrowed" the down payment from him.

Hammond is amazed that Cates would just leave his car out in the open, but Jack

EDDIE MURPHY is released from prison but his trouble has only just begun in ANOTHER 48 HOURS....

tells him to relax as he's installed an alarm system.

He pulls out the key ring and presses the alarm button. Suddenly the Porsche explodes, taking Reggie's remaining $75,000 with it.

A little later, Cates enters the precinct squad room and learns there is no information on who attacked the bus. Then he is grabbed by Captain Haden, who demands he turn over his gun, although Haden acknowledges that Cates has another weapon at home, badge and police I.D. card. He adds that Cates should be more like Kehoe, a good cop that doesn't cause him problems "every two weeks." Cates simply has to learn how to play by the rules.

When Haden walks away, Kehoe suggests that Wilson is getting pressure from above which is why he's trying to get Cates put away. Cates knows that it's personal.

Kehoe notes that there have been three complaints involving bikers. Cates takes the information and turns his attention to the computer.

Kehoe offers his help, pointing out that Cates might not be in such trouble if he were more of a team player.

The computer prints out a composite that looks exactly like Burroughs. Cates hands one of the two copies to Kehoe, asking him to run it through NCIC. Kehoe wants to know who the man in the portrait is, but Cates says that's what he wants to learn and leaves.

He's going to investigate the biker complaints.

Outside, Hammond is talking to a beautiful woman. It seems as though their conversation might lead somewhere, when Cates gets into the car and peels out. As always when these guys are in a car together, the film delivers more characterization. This time, the audience learns that Cates has been dating a female cop named Creal.

Cates has Reggie reach into the glove compartment to remove a "four inch blue .44 magnum" and a plastic police badge, which he believes most people won't be able to tell from the real thing. That night they arrive at a bar, and Cates again asks Ham-

Nick Nolte and EDDIE MURPHY huddle over the phone for ANOTHER 48 HOURS....

mond whether he's going to help.

Reggie responds that he doesn't trust people who screw over their friends and steal their money. They enter and Cates asks the barmaid some questions, as she had called in a complaint regarding bikers who were harassing her.

The woman identifies a photograph of Burroughs, which raises Jack's hopes that this is the man he had seen in the barn. After they leave the bar, he again asks Hammond if he'll help. Realizing he will loose his money and his life if he doesn't, Reggie finally gives him a name. He reveals that Cherry Tilman is one of the bikers who tried to kill him while he was on the bus.

Tilman, a member of the Aryan Brotherhood, was in Folsom with Hammond five years earlier, and tried to kill him then. One of the other convicts "dropped a dime" on Tilman, resulting in the man being placed in solitary confinement. The once useful piece of information he got was that Tilman's wife, Angel Allen, used to perform a live sex act at the Show and Tell strip joint.

When they arrive at the strip club. Hammond goes upstairs to see if Angel is there. Cates serves as look-out.

Hickok and Brother Ed arrive in the alley, and put their cycles next to Cherry's, noting that they hope he hurries. They start up the fire escape, making enough noise that Cates takes notice of them.

He pulls out his gun and starts up the stairs. Hammond, meanwhile, knocks on Angel's door, interrupting her and Cherry. The door opens and he's stunned to see Cherry pulling on his clothes. Both men look at the holstered gun hanging on a chair which is closer to Hammond than to Cherry. Outside the room, Cates catches up to Hickok and has him spread himself against the wall.

In the room, Hammond reaches the gun first, but Cherry leaps over the bed and into the hall.

In the hall, Brother Ed leans in the window, aiming his weapon at Cates and firing. Cates ducks, but the blast gives Hickock a chance to pull his own weapon.

At that moment, Cherry comes running down the stairs with Hammond in pursuit.

Hickock aims his weapon at Reggie and squeezes off two shots.

Cherry and Hickock dive out the window, but Cates blows away Brother Ed. The chase leads outside, where Hickock and Cherry mount their motorcycles and take off, escaping.

Shortly later, Cates receives a report via radio. It's about Brother Ed, and includes the fact that the L.A.P.D. faxed over some material on bikers they've had trouble with.

Cates asks Kehoe to meet him in front of the station in fifteen minutes. Hammond says he'll trust Cates if the cop will drop him off at the home of a girl he knows so he can have some quick sex. Cates agrees, telling him he'll be back in a half an hour.

Hammond heads up to the woman's apartment, and purchases a Glock 9mm. weapon.

Cates drives up to the police station and Kehoe gets in his car just as Wilson calls out to him. The car pulls away, and Kehoe pulls out photos of the bikers they were able to I.D. Cates recognizes Hickock and Cherry, who, Kehoe reveals, are cop killers and are probably putting him at the top of their hit list.

Kehoe suggests that if they should move in, Jack should just take them out rather than do it by the book.

Hammond and Cates reunite, and Reggie is amazed to learn that his "partner" knows he purchased a gun. Hammond suggests that the only way to find the Iceman is to go to Folsom. There they meet with Tyrone Robinson, who Cates pisses off. Reggie restores some calm and Robinson says that a man named Malcolm Price would be the one person who could tell them who put the hit out on Reggie.

The two prepare to leave as Robinson reinforces the idea that Hammond had better live up to his financial commitment. Getting to a pay phone, Cates calls Captain Haden and asks that Creal gather all information on Price. He hangs up before Haden can respond.

The two go to a biker hangout called The Spider Web. There they get into a screaming match, which eventually turns into a fight between Cates and a biker. Several other bikers jump in, and so does Hammond. By the time the fight is over, and our heroes have lost, the biker is so impressed with the way they held their own, he buys them a drink. The biker ultimately gives them Price's address at a local hotel.

As they're driving, the film delivers more exposition. Cates explains that he did go to see Hammond in jail once, but he didn't know what to say. He'd heard how Reggie had continued screwing up and it disappointed him. "I guess I wanted to think different," he says.

Reggie suggests that he could have spoken to him about it and Cates agrees. Cates admits he was wrong. The two, their friendship reaffirmed, proceed after the Iceman.

They arrive at the hotel only to find the clerk murdered. Cates calls the police while Hammond checks the registration book. He learns that Price is in room 317.

Hammond is first in the room, as Cates was delayed in the lobby. He sees Price just before the Iceman comes through the door behind him firing his gun. Hammond barely dives out of the way.

Iceman runs down the corridor and Hammond follows an instant later. The elevator doors open and Cates fires at Iceman, but misses. Eventually the duo pursue their adversary to the large hotel basement, but are too late as Iceman has climbed out the window and driven off.

They make their way outside and are surrounded by cops.

After Cates and Hammond are locked up, Reggie comes to the conclusion that the Iceman is a cop, pointing to the missing gun Cates has searched so hard to find. Considering this, Cates deduces it must be Wilson, as no one investigates the investigators.

The trick is to get out of jail so Hammond can I.D. him. A short while later, Haden uses his clout to get them out, telling Cates he has twenty minutes to get over to his hearing before it means all of their butts.

Cates and Hammond arrive and Jack is stunned to learn that Wilson is _not_ Iceman.

Reggie has never seen him before.

The sequence ends with Cates being fired and a criminal trial date being arranged for him. Later, Cates goes to his locker and withdraws $75,000 which he held back from Hammond in case he needed it for the lawyers. He also informs him that he's got a bondsman. This means Hammond will be getting back his $400,000 dollars in a day or two.

They move outside, with Cates accepting defeat. He offers Reggie a ride, activates his alarm control and the Caddy explodes.

"Say, Jack, where'd you get these alarms put in, anyway?" Hammond asks.

Taking it very well, Cates says he had better go make his final report as a cop. Meanwhile, Hammond goes to a local supermarket, gives the $75,000 to Robinson's daughter, Amy, and tells her that this is her father's last attempt to do something right for her after so many years of doing wrong. Reluctant at first, she accepts the money. Then, pulling him over to the side, she tells him that some Muslims had come to see her earlier and, feeling that he would go to see her father, told her they'd pay $5,000 if she'd tell them where Reggie was. She was supposed to call over to the Cultural Arts Center in the Fillmore district.

Hammond thanks her for the information. In the squad room, Cates and Kehoe discuss the situation, both apparently disgusted. Creal is apologetic that she didn't lay a piece down at the scene for him. He, of course, says that would have been out of the question.

His personal belongings packed, Cates gets ready to leave when Wilson approaches and asks if he's remembered everything. Cates says there's one thing he forgot, and decks the man.

Hammond arrives at the Cultural Arts Center, which in actuality is a pool hall and bar. Identifying himself as Teddy Lemon, Reggie wants to know who he speaks to about Hammond. The Muslim leader, Hakim, pulls a knife and demands to know what information "Teddy" is peddling. Hammond removes the Glock 9mm. and places it against the man's throat, wanting to know where he can find the bikers.

In a sleazy motel, Burroughs, Hickok and Cherry await further instructions from

Iceman. The phone rings and Hickock is told that Hammond will be delivered to them. They proceed to the roof of a parking structure and the Muslims drive up, drop Hammond out of the vehicle and take off.

The men decide to have some fun before killing him, so Cherry starts pummeling him, until Hammond shatters his nose.

At that moment, Iceman steps out of the shadows and tells them to stop playing games and just shoot him.

Cherry goes for his shotgun, but Cates suddenly announces, "I don't think that's gonna happen." His .44 is aimed at Cherry as he steps out of the shadows, telling the masked Iceman to remove his mask.

The man does so, and Hammond announces that he is definitely the person he robbed eight years earlier. The film finally reveals that Iceman is actually Kehoe.

Cates announces that Kehoe never ran the information through NCIC, and that it was he who picked up the gun in the stable. Kehoe chalks it off to having to have more leverage because Jack was getting too close.

An innocent couple step out of the elevator allowing a gunfight to ensue. Cherry and Hickock are killed, thanks mostly to Reggie, and it comes down to Cates and Kehoe holding weapons at each other. They discuss motivations and the struggle between the right and wrong side of the law, but it all ends with Kehoe attempting to shoot him. Cates empties his .44 into Kehoe instead.

The Iceman is dead. Hammond has his money back. Cates will undoubtedly be re-instated. There is no doubt that the boys are back in town!

It is impossible to judge *Another 48 Hrs.* by the screenplay. Still, it is safe to say that audiences will thrill to the magic combination of Eddie Murphy, Nick Nolte and director Walter Hill, just as they did in 1982.

The story itself is not earthshaking, but neither was the original. The strength of *48 Hrs.* came from the fine characterizations, the outrageous dialogue and Hill's frenetic energy as a director. The same elements will work in this film.

Reggie Hammond is not overbearing, as one would have feared considering Mur-

Walter Hill and EDDIE MURPHY during the filming of ANOTHER 48 HOURS....

phy's power in Hollywood. Thankfully, Reggie Hammond and Jack Cates are on equal footing which enhances the film.

It's been eight years since the original, and one can only hope that if there is to be a third "episode", it will be produced in considerably less time.

ANOTHER 48 HOURS finds EDDIE MURPHY as feisty as ever....

□ Filmography....

48 HOURS

CAST

Nick Nolte: Detective Jack Cates
Eddie Murphy: Reggie Hammond
Annette O'Toole: Elaine
Frank McRae: Captain Haden
James Remar: Albert Ganz
David Patrick Kelly: Luther
Sonny Landham: Billy Bear
Brion James: Kehoe
Kerry Sherman: Rosalie
Jonathan Banks: Algren
James Keane: Vanzant
Greta Blackburn: Lisa
Margot Rose: Casey
Denise Crosby: Sally
Olivia Brown: Candy
Todd Allen: Young Cop
Bill Dearth: Thin Cop
Ned Dowd: Big Cop
Jim Haynie: Old Cop
Jack Thibeau: Detective
Jon St: Elwood: Plainclothes Man
Matt Landers: Bob
Peter Jason: Cowboy Bartender
Bill Cross: 1st Cop
Chris Mulkey: 2nd Cop
James Marcelino: Parking Lot Attendant
Walter Scott: Brady
Bennie Dobbins
W: T: Zacha: Road Gang Guards
Begona Plaza: Indian Hooker
Lloyd Catlett
B: G: Bisher
Reid Cruickshanks: Prison Guards
R: D: Call: Duty Sergeant
Brenda Venus
Gloria Gifford: Hookers
Nick Dimitri
John Dennis Johnston
Rock Walker: Torchy Patrons
Dave Moordigan: Gas Station Attendant
J: Wesley Huston: Security Guard
Gary Pettinger: Cop With Gun
Marguerita Wallace
Angela Robinson: Bar Girls
Jack Lightsy: Bartender
John Hauk: Henry Wong
Bob Yanez: Interrogator
Clint Smith: Leroy
Luis Contreras: Gang Member

Suzanne Regard: Cowgirl Dancer
Ola Ray
Bjaye Turner: Vroman's Dancers
Tara King: Frizzy
CREW
Executive Producers: Lawrence Gordon, Joel Silver and D: Constantine Conte
Directed by: Walter Hill
Screenplay by: Roger Spottiswoode, Walter Hill, Larry Gross & Steven E: de Souza
Director of Photography: Ric Waite
Edited by: Freeman Davies, Mark Warner and Bill Weber
Location Manager: Mary Galloway
2nd Assistant Director: Deborah A: Love
Original Music by: James Horner
Music Editor: Michael Tronick
Musical Performers: The Bus Boys ("The Boys Are Back in Town", "48 HRS", "New Shoes"), Kevin O'Neal ("Love Songs Are For Crazies"), Ira Newborn ("Torchy's Boogie") and Sting ("Roxanne")
Production Designer: John Vallone
Set Decorator: Richard Goddard
Special Effects: Joseph P: Mercurio
Costume Designer: Marilyn Vance-Straker
Costume Supervisor: Tom Bronson
Custumes (Men): Dan Moore
Costumes (Women): Jenniver Parsons
Make-up: Michael Germain & Edouard Henriques
Main Title Design: Douy Swofford
Sound Recording (Music): Dan Wallin
Sound Rerecording Mixer: Donald O: Mitchell & Greg Landaker
First Assistant Director: David Sosna
Sound Effects Editor Supervisor: Stephen Hunter Flick, Richard Anderson
Unit Production Manager: Gene Levy
Sound Recording: Glenn Anderson
Assistant Editors: Robert Henandez, Carmel Davies, Edward Warschilka, Jr:
Script Supervisor: Luca Kouimelis
Publicist Coordinator: Rafe Blasi
Stills: Bruce McBroom
Property Master: Craig Raiche
Transportation Coordinator: Ron Baker
Gaffer: Carl Boles
Key Grip: John London
Construction Coordinator: Johnny Lattanzio
Sound: Glenn Anderson
Unit Production Manager: Gene Levy
Distributed by Paramount Pictures
Running Time: 97 mins
Rated: "R"
Released in USA December 1982.

TRADING PLACES

CAST

Dan Aykroyd: Louis Winthorpe III
Eddie Murphy: Billy Ray Valentine
Ralph Bellamy: Randolph Duke
Don Ameche: Mortimer Duke
Denholm Elliot: Coleman
Jamie Lee Curtis: Ophelia
Paul Gleason: Beeks
Kristin Holby: Penelope
Robert Curtis-Brown: Todd
Maurice Woods
Jim Gallagher
Bonnie Behrend
Jim Newell
Bonnie Tremena
Richard D. Fisher Jr.
Anthony DiSabatino
Sunnie Merrilly
Mary St. John
David Schwartz: Duke & Duke Employees
Tom Degidon
Alan Dellay
Ray D'Amore
Herb Peterson
Walt Gorney
William Magerman
Forence Anglin
Bobra Suiter
Sue Dugan
Constance B. Barry: Duke Domestics
Jay P. Sidney: .Heritage Club Doorman
Avon Long: .Ezra
Tom Mardirosian: Officer Pantuzzi
Charles Brown: Officer Reynolds
Nicholas Guest: Harry
John Bedford Lloyd: Andrew
Tony Sherer: Philip
Robert Earl Jones: Attendant
Robert E. Lee: .1st Cop
Peter Hock: .2nd Cop
Clint Smith: .Do Rag Lenny
Ron Taylor: .Big Black Guy
James D. Turner: .Even Bigger Black Guy
Giancarlo Esposito: 2nd Cellmate
Steve Hofvendahl: 3rd Cellmate
James Eckhouse: Guard
Gwyllum Evans: Pres. of Heritage Club
Frank Oz: Corrupt Cop
Eddie Jones: .3rd Cop
John McCurry: 4th Cop

Michele Mais: .1st Hooker
Barra Kahn: 2nd Hooker
Bill Cobbs: Bartender
Bo Diddley: Pawnbroker
CREW
Executive Producers: .Aaron Russo & George Folsey Jr.
Associate Producers: Sam Williams & Irwin Russo
Directed by: John Landis
Screenplay by: Timothy Harris and Herschel Weingrod
Director of Photography: Robert Paynter
Edited by: Malcolm Campbell
Production Designer: .Gene Rudolf
1st Assistant Director: David Sosna
2nd Assistant Directors: Joseph Ray, Linda Montanti and George Folsey, Jr.
Original Music by: Elmer Bernstein
Casting: Bonnie Timmermann
Production Coordinator: Adeline Leonard Seakwood
Unit Production Manager: .William C. Gerrity
Location Manager (Philadelphia): .David Schwartz
Camera Operator (2nd Unit): .Warren Rothenberger
Camera Operators: Richard Kratina, Don Sweeney and Jonathan Fauer
Set Decorators: George DeTitta and George DeTitta, Jr.
Set Dressers: .David Weinman and Anthony Gamiello
Master Scenic Artist: Eugene Powell
Scenic Artists: Bruno Robotti, Leslie Salter-Griffin, William Chaiken
Music: .Wolfgang Amadeus Mozart ("Overture from the Marriage of Figaro", "AndanteCantabile"),
Murray Adler, Harris Goldman, Armand Kaproff ("AndanteCantabile"), Dave Williams ("Out of the
Sheets Into the Streets"), Patrick Cowley & Sylvester ("Do YouWanna Funk"), Nicholas Guest, Robert,
Curtis-Brown, The Hot Toddies ("Oralee Cookies"), Michael Lang, Chuck Domanico, George Doering,
("The Louis Winthorpe III Blues"), Joe Beal, Jim Boothe and Brenda Lee ("Jingle Bell Rock"), Lyn
Murray("The Big Waltz"), Gerry Goffin, Carole King and Eva Little ("The Loco-Motion"), The Sil-
houettes ("Get a Job")
Orchestrations: .Peter Bernstein
Music Editors: .Jeff Carcon, Kathy Durning
Costume Designer: Deborah Nadoolman
Wardrobe (men): William Loger
Wardrobe (women): .Alba Schipani
Costumes: .Guy Tanno
Make-up: .Jack Engel
Titles and Opticals: Modern Film Effects
Sound Editor Supervisor: Charles L. Campbell
Sound Editors: Larry Crutcher, Jerry Stanford, Bruce Richardson, Larry Mann
Sound Recording Mixers: .Frank Grziadei, Dan Wallin, James Sabat, Robert Buzz Knudson, Robert W.
Glass Jr., Don DiGirolamo
Sound Rerecording Facilities: .Todd-AO
Foley Editor: Neil Burrow
Foleys: John Roesch, Joan Rowe
Assistant Editors: Margaret Adachi, Jill Demby, Lorinda Hollingshead, Emily Paine
Stills: .Josh Weiner
Hairstyles: Frank Bianco
Props: Jimmy Raitt
Script Supervisor: Renee Bodner

Key Grip: .Dennis Gamiello
Publicist: .Eric Myers
Distributed by Paramount Pictures
Running Time: 106 minutes
Rating: "R"
Released in USA June 1983.

BEST DEFENSE

CAST

Dudley Moore: Wylie
Eddie Murphy: Landry
Kate Capshaw: Laura
Helen Shaver: Claire
George Dzundza: Loparino
David Rasche: Jeff
Mark Arnott: Brank
Peter Michael Goetz: Joyner
Tom Noonan: Holtzman
Paul Comi: Chief Agent
Darryl Henriques: Colonel Zayas
Joel Polis: 1st Agent
John Zee: Colonel McGuinn
Matthew Laurence: Ali
Christopher Mahar: Sayyid
Lorry Goldman: Rupp
Stoney Richards: Mugger
Tyler Tyhurst: American Captain
Eduardo Richard: Garcia Vega
William Marquez: Padilla
Deborah Fallender: Toni
Raye Birk: Sonny
Ellen Crawford: Sonya
Gene Dynarski: Gil
John Hostetter: Quirk
David Paymer: Kurly
Dennis Redfield: Specs
Jerry Hyman: Colonel Kleinman
Hugo L. Stanger: Blevin
Tracey Ross: Arab Girl
Michael Scalera: Morgan
Rob Wininger: Lieutenant Chapin
Gary Bayer: Lubell
Ronald Salley: Transportation Captain
Paul Eiding: Tourist
Stephen Bradley: Deputy Director
Sanford Jensen: 2nd Engineer
Gerald Jahn: 3rd Engineer
Jennifer Wallace: 1st Waitress
Renny Temple: Coffee Machine Mover
Ziporah Tzabari: Ancient Kuwaiti Woman
Gabi Amrani: Old Villager

Rozsika Hamos: Seamtress
Diane Carter: Technician
Jake Dengel: Doorman
Billy Ray Sharkey: Radio Man
Burton Collins: Cameraman
Bill Geisslinger: Walkie Talkie Agent
Itzhak Bbi Neeman: Refugee Man
Jim Jansen: Lieutenant
Javier Grajeda: Freddie Gomez
Patricia Pivaar: Female Newscaster
Julie Ellis: 2nd Waitress
Yulius Ruval: French Singer
Pamela Stonebrook: Singer
Elizabeth Kubota: Japanese Singer
Rick Dees: Himself
Commander Chuck Street: Himself

CREW
Produced by: Katz-Huyck Productions
Producer: Gloria Katz
Directed by: Willard Huyck
Screenplay by: Gloria Katz& William Huyck
Based on the Novel by: Robert Grossbach
Director of Photography: Don Peterman
Edited by: Michael A: Stevenson, Sidney Wolinsky
Production Designer: Peter Jamison
Art Direction: Robert W: Welch III
Set Decorator: Chris R: Westlund
Original Music by: Patrick Williams
Casting: Dianne Crittenden
Costume Designer: Kristi Zea
Additional Editing: Billy Weber
Unit Production Manager: Austen Jewell, Robert Latham Brown
1st Assistant Director: Jerry Grandey
2nd Assistant Director: Catherine Wanek
Special Effects: Richard E: Johnson, John R: Elliot
Camera Operator: Keith Peterman
Camera Operator 1st Assistant: John E: LeBlanc
Camera Operator 2nd Assistant: John C: Moulds
Gaffer: Wright K: Manning
Key Grip: Gerald A: King
Set Designer: Don Woodruff, Joseph Nemec III
Construction Coordinator: Robert Krume
Property Master: Steven R: Westlund
Script Supervisor: Louise Jaffe
Location Manager: Brian Brosnan
Production Auditor: Sandra Rabins
Moldmaker: George Samson
Production Illustrator: John C: Johnson Jr:
Sound Mixer: Jerry Jost
Boom Operator: Pat Suraci
Music Editor Supervisor: Richard Stone
Music Editor: Segue Music

Running Time: 94 Minutes
Rated: "R"
Distributed by Paramount Pictures

BEVERLY HILLS COP

CAST

Eddie Murphy: Axel Foley
Judge Reinhold: Detective Billy Rosewood
Lisa Eilbacher: Jenny Summers
John Ashton: Segeant Taggart
Ronny Cox: Lieutenant Bogomil
Steven Berkoff: Victor Maitland
James Russo: Mikey Tandino
Jonathan Banks: Zack
Stephen Elliot: Chief Hubbard
Gilbert R Hill: Inspector Todd
Art Kimbro: Detective Foster
Joel Bailey: Detective McCabe
Bronson Pinchot: Serge
Paul Reiser: Jeffrey
Michael Champion: Casey
Frank Pesce: Cigarette Buyer
Gene Borkan: Truck Driver
Michael Gregory: Hotel Manager
Alice Cagogan: Hotel Clerk
Philip Levien: Donny
Karen Mayo-Chandler: Maitland Receptionist
Gerald Berns: 1st Beverly Hills Cop
William Wallace: 2nd Beverly Hills Cop
Israel Juarbe: Room Service Waiter
Randy Gallion: Bell Hop
Damon Wayans: Banana Man
Chuck Adamson: 1st Crate Opener
Chip Heller: 2nd Crate Opener
Rich Overton: Bonded Warehouse Night Supervisor
Rex Ryon: Bonded Warehouse Security Guard
Michael Pniewski: 1st Bonded Warehouse Clerk
Douglas Warhit: 2nd Bonded Warehouse Clerk
Paul Drake: 1st Holdup Man
Tom Everett: 2nd Holdup Man
Sally Kishbaugh: Waitress
Barry Shade: Valet
Jack Heller: Harrow Club Maitre D'
Michael Harrington: Harrow Club Arresting Officer
David Wells: Dispatcher
Scott Murphy: Detective Owenby
Dennis Madden: 1st Detroit Station Cop
Carl Weintraub: 2nd Detroit Station Cop
Anthony DeFonte: 3rd Detroit Station Cop
Darwyn Carson: Barmaid
Mark E Corry: Pool Player

Thomas J Hageboeck: Maitland Bodyguard
CREW
Executive Producers: Don Simpson and Jerry Bruckheimer
Produced by: Mike Moder
Associate Producer: Linda Horner
Directed by: Martin Brest
Screenplay by: Daniel Petrie Jr
Story by: Daniel Petrie Jr and Danilo Bach
Director of Photography: Bruce Surtees
Editors: Billy Weber and Arthur Coburn
Production Designer: Angelo Graham
Unit Production Manager: Mike Moder
Location Managers: James Herbert, William Bowling and Robert Decker
2nd Unit Director: Thomas Wright
Assistant Directors: Peter Bogart and Richard Graves
Assistant 2nd Unit Director: Steve McRoberts
Camera Operator: Jack Green
2nd Camera Operator: Jeffrey L Miller
Art Direction: James J Murakami
Set Decorator: Jeff Haley and John M Dwyer
Gallery Artwork: Peter Gebhardt, Paul Mogensen, Gary Gibson, Bruce Richards, Eugene Jardin, John Sonsini, Larry Lubow, Don Sorensen, Andre Mirapolski, Rita Yokoi and Simon Doonan
Special Effects: Ken Pepiot
Sound Editor (Music): Bob Badami
Costume Designer: Tom Bronson
Costumes: Kathleen Gale, Micael Long and Chuck Velasco
Makeup: Ben Nye Jr and Leonard Engelman
Title Design: R/Greenberg Associates
Sound Editor Supervisors: Cecelia Hall and George Watters II
Sound Editors: Teri E Dorman, Bruce Lacey and Paul Bruce Richardson
ADR Editor: Alan Nineberg
Foley Editor: Pamela Bentkowski and Alan Bromberg
Sound Recording: Charles Wilborn and Gary Ritchie
Sound Rerecording: Donald O Mitchell, Gregg Landaker and Rick Kline
Digital Consultant: Brian Reeves
Technical Consultant: Chuck Adamson
Computer Effects Consultant: Steve Grumette
Stunt Coordinator: Gary McLarty
Script Supervisor: Matt Johnston
Key Grip: Peter Wagner
Unit Publicist: Stanley Brossette
Produced by Paramount Pictures, Don Simpson-Jerry Bruckheimer and Eddie Murphy Productions
Running Time: 105 Minutes
Rating: "R"

THE GOLDEN CHILD

CAST

Eddie Murphy: Chandler Jarrell
Charles Dance: Sardo Numspa
Charlotte Lewis: Kee Nang
Victor Wong: The Old Man
Randall "Tex" Cobb: Til
James Hong: Doctor Hong
Shakti: Kala
Tau Logo: Yu
Tiger Chung Lee: Khan
Pons Maar: Fu
Peter Kwong: Tommy Tong
Wally Taylor: Detective Boggs
Eric Douglas: Yellow Dragon
Charles Levin: TV Host
Kenneth "Fruitty" Frith, Jr: Friend at Pink's
Bennett Ohta: Herb Shop Clerk
Tscubouchi Kinko: Old Chinese Woman
Govind Chipalu: Jabbering Old Man
Chantara Nop: 1st Security Man
Ok Phok: 2nd Security Man
Bob Tzudiker: Businessman
Cliffy Magee: Russell
Jeff Soo Hoo: Waiter
Bindra Joshi: Chicken Lady on Plane
Judy Hudson: Tortoise Lady
Ron Packham: Buttonman
Marilyn Schreffler: Voice of Kala
Frank Welker: Voice of the Thing
JL Reate: The Golden Child

CREW

Executive Producers: Richard Tienken and Charles R Meeker
Co-Producers: Edward S Feldman, Robert D Wachs and Dennis Feldman
Associate Producer: Gordon A Webb
Directed by: Michael Ritchie
Screenplay by Dennis Feldman
Director of Photography: Donald E Thorin
Editor: Richard A harris
Production Designer: J Michael Riva
Original Music by: Michael Colombier
Special Effects: Industrial Light and Magic
Costume Designer: Wayne Finkelman
Casting: Patricia Mock
Unit Production Manager: Gordon A Webb
1st Assistant Director: Tom Mack
2nd Assistant Director: Emmett-Leon O'Neill
Visual Effects Superviser: Ken Ralston
Makeup Creation: Ken Chase
Art Director: Lynda Paradise
Set Decorator: Marvin March

Visual Effects Coordinator: Pamela Easley
Camera Operator: Rob Hahn
Camera Operator 1st Assistant: Don Gold and Donald E Thorin, Jr
Camera Operator 2nd Assistant: Marc Staton
Camera Loader: Jeffrey Thorin
Sound Mixer: Jim Alexander
Boom Operator: Gregg Agalsoff and Gary Thread
Script Supervisor: Marshall Schlom
2nd Assistant Director: W Alexander Ellis
Key Makeup: Steve LaPorte
Hairstyles: Susan Kalinowski
Costume Supervisor: Eddie Marks
Key Costumer (Women): Shari Feldman
Key Costumer (Men): Jim Lapidus
Costumers: Chuck Velasco and Antonio Martinez
Property Master: Barry Bedig
Property Master Assistants: Gary Kieldrup and Ken Orme
Lighting Technician Chief: James Boyle
Chief Lighting Technician Assistants: Ed Nedin and Murphy Wiltz
1st Company Grip: Dan Jordan
2nd Company Grips: Joe Hicks, Edmond Wright and Al Contreras
Dolly Grip: Don Schmitz and Michael Chaney
Animal Trainer: Paul Calabria, Karin Dew, Roland Raffler and Sled Reynolds
Location Manager: Ira Rosenstein
Art Direction Assistant: Cameron Birnie
Set Designer: Virginia Randolph and Judy Cammer
Technical Adviser: Tim Boxell
Production Illustrators: John Johnson and Tom Southwell
Construction Coordinators: George Stokes
Construction Supervisors: James Orendorff and John Clayton
Stunt Coordinator: Chuck Waters
Music Editor Supervisor: Jeff Gilbert and Mike F Carson
Music Editing: Segue Music
Music Scoring Mixers: Dan Wallin and Frank Wolf
Sound Rerecording Mixers: Robert J Litt, Gregg Landaker and Elliot Tyson
Music Recording: Record Plant Scoring
Production Office Coordinator: Barbara Spitz
Production Secretary: Joan Lee Smith
Production Auditor: Ellen Adolph
Production Auditor Assistant: Dennis Park
Casting Consultant (Great Britain): Mary Selway
Casting Consultant (USA): Melissa Skoff
Casting Assistant: Carol Lefko
Unit Publicist: Stan Brossette
Stills: Bruce Talamon
Greensperson: Jess Anscott
Craft Services: Emin Aljuwani
Welfare Worker: Phil Trocki
Assistant to Michael Ritchie: Sue Brooks
Assistant to Edward S Feldman: Alexandra Brouwer
Assistant to Robert D Wachs: Robin Robinson
Assistant to Dennis Feldman: Judy Whelchel

Production Assistants: George McDowell, Leslie Warren, Kenneth Frith Jr, Fetteroff F Colen, Frank Davis and Joseph Brown
Titles and Opticals: Boss Film Corporation
Negative Cutting: MGM Negative Cutting
Color Timer: Ron Lambert
Weapons Consultant: Dan Curry
Technical Adviser (Monastary): Ken McLeod
Demon Props: Chris Walas, Inc
Additional Animation: Available Light, LTD
Panaflex Cameras and Lenses: Panavision
Distributed by Paramount Pictures in Assocation With Eddie Murphy Productions
Running Time: 94 Minutes
Rating: "PG-13"

BEVERLY HILLS COP II
CAST
Eddie Murphy: Axel Foley
Judge Reinhold: Billy Rosewood
Jurgen Prochnow: Maxwell Dent
Ronny Cox: Andrew Bogomil
John Ashton: John Taggart
Brigitte Nielsen: Karla Fry
Allen Garfield: Harold Lutz
Dean Stockwell: Chip Cain
Paul Reiser: Jeffrey Friedman
Gil Hill: Inspector Todd
Paul Guilfoyle: Nikos Thomopolis
Robert Ridgley: Mayor Egan
Peggy Sands: Stripper
Larry Carroll: TV Reporter
Carlos Cervantes: Mendoza
Michael DeMarlo: Doorman at Adirano's
Dana Gladstone: Francesco
Richmond Harrison: Construction Worker
Darryl Henriques: Maitre D' at 385
John Hostetter: Stiles
Tom "Tiny" Lister Jr: Orvis
Ed Pansullo: Ailey
Rudy Ramos: Ignacio
Ritch Shydner: Guard at Hef's
John Lisbon Wood: Bobby Morgan
Carl Bringas
Joe Duquette
Michael Hehr
Sam Sako: Bodyguards
Michael F Kelly: Guard at Gate
William Lamar
Christopher R Adams
Danny Nero
Devin Bartlett: Thugs
Dayna O'Brien: Girl at Club

Eugene Mounts: Policeman
Everett Sherman Jr: Man at Street Corner
Catrin Cole: Vinnie's girl
Ola Ray
Alana Soares
Venice Kong
Luann Lee
Rebecca Ferratti
Kymberly Paige
Kymberly Herrin: Playboy Playmates
Leilani Soares
Anne Lammot
Pamela Santini
Sarah Quick
Marlenne Kingsland
Monet Swann
Natalie Smith
Kari Whitman: Playboy Models

CREW
Executive Producers: Robert D Wachs, Richard Tienken, Don Simpson, Jerry Bruckheimer
Directed by: Tony Scott
Screenplay by: Larry Ferguson and Warren Skaaren
Story by: Eddie Murphy and Robert D Wachs
Based on Characters Created by: Danilo Bach and Daniel Petrie Jr
Director of Photography: Jeffrey L Kimball
Edited by: Chris Lebenzon and Michael Tronick
Production Designer: Ken Davis
Unit Production Manager: Arthur Seidel
1st Assistant Director: Peter Bogart
2nd Assistant Director: Hope Goodwin
Art Director: James J Murakami
John H Anderson: Set Decorator
Camera Operators: Michael A Benson and Charles E Mills Anderson
Camera Operator 1st Assistant: Aaron Panzanti and Greg Schmidt
Camera Operator 2nd Assistant: Robert B Samuels and Mart Staton
Stills: Bruce W Talamon
Sound Recording Mixer: William B Kaplan
Sound Editor Supervisors: Cecelia Hall and George Watters II
Sound Editors: Marshall Winn, Barbara McBane, Frank Howard, Kimberly Harris, Victor Grodecki, Julia Evershade and Marty Nicholson
ADR Editor Supervisor: Juno J Ellis
ADR Editor: Dick Darling
Foley Editor Supervisor: Pamela Bentkowski
Foley Editors: Bruce Fortune and Joey Ippolito
Assistant Editors: Claudia Finkle, Peter N Lonsdale and Carolyn Fitzgerald
Apprentice Editors: Darrell Upshaw and Craig Nelson
Sound Recording Mixers: Donald O Mitchell, Rick Kline and Kevin O'Connell
Sound Editor Assistants: Judee Gustafson, Daniel F Finnerty and Irene Bennett
Sound Effects Recordist: John Paul Fasal
Sound Editor Apprentice: Paul Lestz
Production Office Coordinator: Yvonne Yaconelli
Production Adminstrator to Simpson & Bruckheimer: Kathryn Anderson

Assistant to Don Simpson: Monica Harmon
Assistant to Jerry Bruckheimer: Ginger Reynolds and David J Robertson
Assistant to Robert D Wachs & Richard Tienken: Marilyn Gill-Trenkle
Assistant (Eddie Murphy Productions): Patricia Matthews
Assistant to Tony Scott: Catalaine Knell
Secretary to Tony Scott: Lisa G Shillinburg
Production Assistant: Scott Metcalfe
Assistants to Producer: Charles Murphy, Ray Murphy, Sr, Kenneth Frith, Jr, Darlene Jackson and Kurt Davis
Makeup: Steve Abrums, Ellen Wong and Mario Gonzales
Hairstyles: Dorothea Long and Eddie Barron
Personal Consultant (Brigitte Nielsen): Anthony Clavet
Costume Supervisor: James Tyson
Wardrobe: Gary R Sampson, Fetteroff Colen, Cha Blevins and Janice Mekaelian
Location Managers: Bruce Lawhead and Jack English
Location Manager Assistant: Robert Doyle
Art Direction Assistant: Cate Bangs
Property Master: Mike Blaze and Tommy Tomlinson
Property Master Assistant: Larry Johnson
Property Leadperson: Mike Higelmire
Set Designer Leadperson: Henry Alberti, David Klassen and Mark Fabus
Illustrator: Sherman Labby
Construction Foreperson: Mark Lawrence
Production Painter: James Ecker
Production Auditor: Allen Adolph
Production Auditor Assistant: Tony Criscione
Production Secretary: Susie Mitchell
Casting: Bonnie Timmermann and Vickie Thomas
Casting Assistant: Aleta Wood-Chappelle, Jeffrey Block and Renee Milliken
Unit Publicist: Marsha Robertson
Publicity: Peggy Siegal Company
Chief Lighting Technician: Ward Russell
Chief Lighting Technician Assistant: Dan Delgado and Edward Reily
Electrical Lighting Technician: Eddie Taylor
1st Company Grip: Thomas Prophet Jr
2nd Company Grip: Larry Sweet and Jay Davis
Dolly Grip: J Michael Popovich
Boom Operator: Earl F Sampson
Utility Sound Technican: Steve Klinghoffer
Stunt Coordinator: Gary McLarty and Alan Oliney
Special Effects Supervisor: Tom Ryba
Special Effects Assistants: Dave Blitstein, Tom Tokunaga and Johnny Borgese
Special Laser Effects: Laser Media Inc
Transportation Coordinator: Leroy Reed
Transportation Captains: Mike Antunez and Mario Perez
DGA Trainee: Adele Simmons
Technical Advisor (Police): TJ Hageboeck
Computer Consultants: Steve Grummett and Roger Switzer
Greensperson: Richard Landau
Music Consultant (MCA Records): Kathy Nelson
Music Editor: Bob Badami
First Aid: Ron Eisenman

Craft Service: Emin Aljuwani
Caterer: Tony Kerum (Tony's Food Service)
Production Assistant: Cherie Bailey and Charlotte Lestern
Negative Cutting: Reel People, Inc
Color Timer: Dick Ritchie
Titles and Opticals: Cinema Research Corporation
Title Design: Dan Curry
Assistance: Detroit Police Department
Distributed by Paramount Pictures
Running Time: 102 Minutes
Rated: "R"

COMING TO AMERICA
CAST
Eddie Murphy: Prince Akeem, Clarence, Saul and Randy Watson
Arsenio Hall: Semmi, Morris, Extremely Ugly Girl and Reverend Brown
James Earl Jones: King Jaffe Joffer
Madge Sinclair: Queen Aoleon
John Amos: Cleo McDowell
Allison Dean: Patrice McDowell
Shari Headley: Lisa McDowell
Eriq LaSalle: Darryl Jenks
Paul Bates: Oha
Garcelle Beavais
Feather
Stephanie Simon: Rose Bearers
Victoria Dillard
Felicia Taylor
Michele Watley: Bathers
Sheila Johnson: Lady-in-Waiting
Raymond D Turner: T-Shirt Hawker
Calvin Lockhart: Colonel Izzi
Billi Gordon: Large Woman
Vanessa Bell: Imani Izzi
Jake Steinfeld: Cab Driver
Cuba Gooding Jr: Boy Getting Haircut
Clint Smith: Sweets
Frankie Faison: Landlord
Uncle Ray Murphy: Stu
Ruben Hudson: Street Hustler
Paulette Banoza: Soul Glo Woman
Clyde R Jones: Soul Glo Man
Patricia Matthews: Devil Woman
Mary Bond Davis: Big Stank Woman
Kara Young: Stuck-Up Girl
Carla Earle: Tough Girl
Karen Renee Owens
Sharon Reneed Owens: Ex-Siamese Twins
Lisa Gumora: Kinky Girl
June Boykins: Strange Woman
Janette Colon: Fresh Peaches

Vanessa Colon: Sugar Cube
Monique Mannen: Boring Girl
Mindora Mimms
Cynthia Finkley: Awareness Women
Louie Anderson: Maurice
David Sosna: Cartier Delivery Man
Vondie Curtis-Hall: Basketball Game Vendor
Samuel L Jackson: Hold-Up Man
Dottie: Dottie the Dog
Arthur Adams: Mr Jenks
Loni Kaye Harkless: Mrs Jenks
Montrose Hagins: Grandma Jenks
Tonja Rivers: Party Guest
Don Ameche: Mortimer Duke
Ralph Ballamy: Randolph Duke
Elaine Kagan: Telegraph Lady
Michael Tadross: Taxi Driver
Steve White: Subway Guy
Helen Hanft: Subway Lady
Birdie M Hale: Elderly Passenger
Jim Abrahams: Face on Cutting Room Floor
Leah Aldridge
Paula Brown
Stephanie Clark
Robin Dimension
Eric L Ellis
Aurorah Allain
Dwayne Chattman
Victoria Dillard
Shaun Earl
Sharon Ferrol
Eric D Henderson
Debra L Johnson
Jimmy Locust
Karen Renee Owens
Donna M Perkins
Gina Consuela Rose
Robbin Tasha-Ford
Eyan Williams
Gigi Hunter
Tanya Lynne Lee
Monique Mannen
Sharon Renee Owens
Dionne Rockhold
Randolph Scott
Jerald Vincent: Dancers

CREW

Executive Producers: Mark Lipsky and Leslie Belzberg
Associate Producer: David Sosna
Produced by: George Folsey Jr and Robert D Wachs
Directed by: John Landis
Screenplay by: David Sheffield and Barry W Balustein

Story by: Eddie Murphy
Director of Photography: Woody Omens
Editors: Malcom Campbell and George Folsey Jr
Music by: Nile Rodgers
Production Designer: Richard MacDonald
Unit Production Manager: William Watkins and Michael Tadross
1st Assistant Director: David Sosna
2nd Assistant Director: Richard Patrick
Costume Designer: Deborah Nadoolman
Special Make-up: Rick Baker
Casting: Jackie Burch
Choreography: Paula Abdul
Special Visual Effects: Syd Dutton and Bill Taylor
Script Supervisor: Luca Kouimelis
Camera Operator Assistants: Phil Caplan and Douglas H Knapp
Camera Operator 1st Assistant: John Szajner and Ken Fisher
Camera Operator 2nd Assistant: Joseph Cosko Jr and Ned Martin
Stills: Bruce McBroom
Unit Publicist: Saul Kahan
2nd Assistant Director: Tracy Rosenthal and Tomaz Remel
DGA Trainee: Michael-McCloud Thompson
Art Direction: Richard Lewis
Art Direction Assistant: Carole Lee Cole
Set Designer: Greg Papalia, Ron Yates, Gil Clayton, Erin Cummins, Larry Hubbs and Cheryal Kearney
Leadman: Randy Bostic
Swing Gang: Lou Mugavero, John Lewis, Greng Lynch & Richard Evans
Sound Recording Mixer: William B Kaplan
Boom Operator: Earl Sampson
Utility Sound/Cable Operator: Randy McDonald
Chief Lighting Technician: Norman Glasser
Chief Lighting Technician Assistants: Ed Cooper and Christopher Whitman
Chief Rigging Electrician: Steve Shaver and Franco Valdez
1st Company Grip: Dennis Harper
2nd Company Grip: Kip Wurl
Dolly Grip: Jon Falkengren and Bud Howell
Property Master: Gregg H Bilson
Property Master Assistants: Stan W Cockerell, Kenny Swenson Jr and Guy Owens
Special Effects Supervisor: Dan Cangemi
Costume Designer Assistant: Kelly Kimball
Costume Supervisor: Francine Jamison-Tanchuck
Key Costumer (Men): Frank Perry Rose
Chief Costumer (Women): Violette Jones-Faison
Costumer: Hugo Pena, Melissa Franz and David Page
Makeup Supervisor: Bernadine Anderson
Makeup Assistants: Marie Carter and Robin Levine
Makeup (Body): Jane English
Hairstyles Supervisor: Robert L Stevenson
Hairstyles Assistant: Bill Howard
Special Makeup: Greg Nelson, Margaret Beserra, Norman Cabrera, Bill Fletcher, Jim Leonard, Greg
Punchantz and Matt Rose
Production Accountant: Janet Wattles
Production Accountant Assistant: Carole Wattles

Production Financial Consultant: James Turner
Assistant Editors: Walter A Hekking and John A Haggar
Apprentice Editor: Markus A Schuab
ADR Editor Supervisor: James Beshears and Leigh French
Sound Rerecording Facilities: Todd-AO/Glen Glenn Studios
Sound Rerecording Mixers: Larry Stensvold and William Gazecki
Music Editor: Daniel Allen Carlin
Music Scoring Mixer: Ed Cherney
Orchestrations: Mark McKenzie
Music Recording Facilities: Record Plant Scoring
Sound Editor Supervisors: Richard C Franklin Jr & Paul Timothy Carden
Sound Editors: Mike Dobie, Lenny Geschke, Donald J Malouf & Charles E Smith
Sound Editor Assistants: Spike Allison Hooper & Pamela G Kimber
Sound Processing: Mel Neiman
Foley Mixer: Dean Drabin
Foley: Gary Hecker and Dan O'Connell
Production Coordinator: Debbie Schwab
Production Secretary: Ginny Warner
Casting Assistant: Ferne Cassel
Casting (Extras): Jim Green and Eddie Smith
Choreography Assistant: Cindy Montoya and Aurorah Allain
Assistant to Robert Wachs & Mark Lipsky: Marilyn Gill-Trenkle
Assistant to Eddie Murphy: Patricia Matthews
Location Manager: Steven Shkolnik
Construction Coordinator: Jerry Fitzpatrick
Main Title Lettering: Douy Swofford
Chief Modelmaker: Grant McCune
Negative Cutting: Reel People, Inc
Color Timer: Bob Nolan
Opticals: Cinema Research Corporation
Panaflex Cameras and Lenses: Panavision
Stunt Coordinator: John Sherrod
Produced by Paramount Pictures in Association With Eddie Murphy Productions
Running Time: 117 Minutes
Rating: "R"

HARLEM NIGHTS
CAST
Eddie Murphy: Mr EM Quick
Richard Pryor: Sugar Ray
Redd Foxx: Bennie Wilson
Danny Aiello: Phil Cantone
Michael Lerner: Bugsy Calhoune
Della Reese: Vera
Berlinda Tolbert: Annie
Stan Shaw: Jack Jenkins
Jasmine Guy: Dominique LaRue
Vic Polizos: Richie Vento
Lela Rochon: Sunshine
David Marciano: Tony
Arsenio Hall: Crying Man

Tommy Ford: Tommy Smalls
Uncle Ray: Willie
Michael Goldfinger: Max
Joe Pecoraro: Joe Leoni
Robin Harris: Jerome
Charles Q Murphy: Jimmy
Miguel Nunez: Man With Broken Nose
Desi Arnez Hines II: Young Quick
Ji-Tu Cumbuka: Toothless Gambler
J Kennedy Horne
Bobby McGee
Reynaldo Rey
Nick Savage: Gamblers
Johnny Smith: Huge Man
Robin Lynn Reed: Woman Employee
Tyrone Granderson Jones
Dan Tullis Jr
Don Blakely
Chris Jackson
Roy L Jones
Howard "Sandman" Sims
Roger E Reid: Crapshooters
Rudy Challenger
Steve White
Dexter A Wilkins
Nona M Gaye: Patrons
Bill Batman: Orderly
Kathleen Bradley: Lady
Clarence Ladnry: Old Man
Carmen Filpi: Dorman
Alvin Silver: Headwaiter
Cliff Strong: Man in Front Seat
Margaret Wheeler: Elderly Woman
Joe Litlefield: Elderly Man
Ricky Aiello: 1st Man
Donald Nardini: 2nd Man
Robert Vento: Bartender
Mike Genovese: Desk Sergeant
Dennis Lee Kelly
William Utay: Cops
Michael Buffer: Announcer
Marc Figueroa: One of Calhoune's Boys
George Kyle: Man at Bugsy's
Eugene R Glazer: Detective Hogan
Michael Stroka: Detective Simms
Eddie Smith: Driver
Gene Hartline: Michael Kirkpatrick
Karen Armstead: Bennie's Girlfriend
Lezley Price: Nurse
Randy Harris: Todo La Noche
Ringside Announcer: Woody Omens
Don Familton: Referee

Dennis kemper: Bathroom Attendent
Larry L Johnson: King Blue
Prince C Spencer: Himself
Roberto Duran: Himself

CREW

Executive Producer: Eddie Murphy
Producers: Robert D Wachs, Mark Lipsky and Ralph S Singleton
Associate Producer: Ray Murphy, Jr
Written and Directed by: Eddie Murphy
Director of Photography: Woody Omens
Editor: George Bowers
Music: Herbie Hancock
Production Designer: Lawrence G Paull
Art Direction: Martin G Hubbard and Russell B Crone
Set Decorator: George R Nelson
Costume Designer: Joe I Tompkins
Unit Production Manager: Ralph S Singleton
1st Assistant Director: Alan B Curtiss
2nd Assistant Directors: Barry K Thomas, John C Rusk, Dorothy A Steinicke and Karen Ginsberg
Casting: Robi Reed
Script Supervisor: Pamela M Alch
Camera Operators: Philip Caplan and Norman G Langley
Camera Operator 1st Assistant: John Z Szajner & Richard A Mention III
Camera Operator 2nd Assistant: Joseph Cosko Jr & Ricardo Robinson
Stills: Bruce Talamon
Art Direction Assistant: Craig D Egar and Jack B Jennings
Set Designer: Alan S Kaye
Production Illustrator (Primary): Mentor Huebner
Storyboard Artist: David Russell
Unit Publicist: Stanley Brossette
Sound Mixer: Gene S Cantemessa
Boom Operator: Steve Cantamessa
Cable Operator: Mark Jennings
Video Assistant: Lindsay P Hill
Chief Lighting Technican: Norman Glasser
Chief Lighting Technician Assistant: Edward Cooper
Chief Rigging Electrician: Steve Shaver
Electrician: Tom Embree, Lloyd Gowdy, Frank Jones, Don Lewis & Scott McKnight
1st Company Grip: Carmon "Bud" Howell
2nd Company Grip: Burton Lindemoen
Dolly Grip: John Falkengren and Bryn Boyd
Grip: Art Mack, John Nettles and Kip Wurl
Property Master: Jimmie Herron
Property Master Assistant: Carey Harris Jr and Renita Lorden
Leadman: Dennis J Vannatta
Props: Jim Greenspan, Ron Sica, Craig Staley, William Timmerman and Ronnie Sue Wexler
Special Effects Supervisor: Chuck Gaspar
Special Effects Foreman: Peter H Albiez
Costume Designer Assistant: Violette Jones Faison
Key Costumer: Norman A Burza and Andrea E Weaver
Makeup: Bernadine M Anderson
Makeup Assistant: Marie Carter and Anthony S Lloyd

Hairstyles: Robert S Stevenson
Hairstyles Assistant: Don Lynch
Production Auditor: Don Petrie
Production Auditor Assistant: Jeanine Wilson and Harry S Knapp
Accounting Assistant: Kim McLaren
Production Office Coordinator: Barbara A Rosing and Tom C Pietzman
Production Secretary: Caryn E Campbell
Casting Associate: Chemin Sylvia Barnard
Casting Assistant: Maria Martin
Stunt Coordinator: Alan Oliney
Location Manager: Anthony J Saenz, Stephen C Dawson, Rene Botana, and James M Morris
Period Research: Karen Ginsberg
Editor (Research): Alan Balsam
Associate Editor: Christopher Koefoed
Assistant Editors: James C Johnson and Joe Gutowski
Apprentice Editor: Rodney Sharpp and Kelly Tartan
Sound Editor Supervisors: John Benson and Cecelia Hall
Sound Editors: Beth Sterner, RJ Palmer, F Hudson Miller, Bruce Fortune, Frank Howard
ADR Editor Supervisor: Fred Stafford
ADR Editor: Juno Ellis
Foley Editor Supervisor: Victoria Martin
Foley Editor: Pam Betkwoski
Sound Editor Assistants: Donald Ortiz and Craig Sims
Music Editor: Bunny Andrews
Music Editor Assistant: Lise Richardson
Foley Artist: Ken Dufva and David Lee Fein
Foley Mixer: Greg Curda
Sound Rerecording Mixers: Michael Casper, Thomas Gerard& Daniel Leahy
Music Recording Consultant: Bob Schaper
Orchestrations & Conductor: Garnett Brown
Music Recording Facilities: Record Plant Scoring
Creative Assistant to Herbie Hancock: David Blumberg
Construction Coordinators: Clarence Lynn Price
Construction Foremen: Robert Carlyle, Ray Rarick, Scott Mason & Neil Saiger
Paint Foremen: Mark Konkel, Wayne Smith, Ron Ashmore, Gerry Gates Sr and Ward Welton
Plasterer: Mike Carroll
Labor Foreman: Ron Schroeder
Sign Writer: Harold D Hinzo and Fred Seibly
Transportation Coordinator: Thomas Hoke
Transportation Captain: Edward Baken
Picture Car Captain: Steve Bonner
Motor Officer Coordinator: Jack Wood
Craft Service: Tom Jones
Caterer: For Stars Catering
Assistant to Eddie Murphy: Desiree DaCosta
Assistant to Robert D Wachs and Mark Lipsky: Yvonne Bonitto Doggett
Office Manager (Eddie Murphy Productions): Leroy Murphy
Assistant to Richard Pryor: Jennie Johnson
Production Assistants: Fetteroff Colen, Dianne Farrington, Michael Green, Nicholas Gross, Randy Harris, Jerome Holmes, Carolyn McLaurin, Julie McNulty, Matthew Unger and Monika Woodward
Negative Cutting: Reel People, Inc
Color Timer: Bob Noland

Opticals: Cinema Research Corporation
Title Design: Neal Thompson
Panaflex Cameras and Lenses: Panavision
Cranes and Dollies: Chapman
Musco Light Technician: Roger Spurgeon
Assistance: Rocco Gioffre, Aaron Siskind, Tania G Werbizky, Preservation League of New York and
Color Me Bright
Distributed by Paramount Pictures in Association With Eddie Murphy Productions
Running Time: 115 Minutes
Rated: "R"

ANOTHER 48 HRS.

CAST
Eddie Murphy: Reggie Hammond
Nick Nolte: Detective Jack Cates
Frank McRae: Captain Haden
Brion James: Kehoe

CREW
Executive Producers: Lawrence Gordon, Robert D Wachs, Mark Lipsky, Ralph Singleton
Co-producer: D Constantine Conte
Associate Producer: Ray Murphy, Jr and Kenneth Frith
Directed by Walter Hill
Screenplay by: Jeb Stuart, John Fasano and Larry Gross
Story by: Eddie Murphy
Director of Photography: Matthew F Leonetti
Production Designer: Joseph Nemec
Editor: Freeman Davies
Unit Production Manager: Ralph Singleton
Assistant Director: James R Dyer
Costumes: Dan Moore
Set Decorator: George R Nelson
Sound Recording Mixer: Willie D Burton

The World's Only
Official

COUCH POTATO BOOK CATALOG ™

Please note:
You must be a certified couch potato* to partake of this offering!

* To become a certified couch potato you must watch a minimum of 25 hours a day at least 8 days per week.

From Happy Hal...

Star Trek
Gunsmoke
The Man from U.N.C.L.E.

They all evoke golden memories of lost days of decades past. What were you doing when you first saw them?

Were you sitting with your parents and brothers and sisters gathered around a small set in your living room?

Were you in your own apartment just setting out on the wonders of supporting yourself, with all of the many associated fears?

Or were you off at some golden summer camp with all of the associated memories, of course forgetting the plague of mosquitoes and the long, arduous hikes?

The memories of the television show are mixed with the memories of the time in a magical blend that always brings a smile to your face. Hopefully we can help bring some of the smiles to life, lighting up your eyes and heart with our work...

Look inside at the **UNCLE Technical Manual**, the **Star Trek Encyclopedia, The Compleat Lost in Space** or the many, many other books about your favorite television shows!

Let me know what you think of our books.

And what you want to see.

It's the only way we can share our love of the wonders of the magic box....

Selection

HAL SCHUSTER

Administration

JACK SCHUSTER, COUCH POTATO

Customer Service

PHYLLIS SCHUSTER

From The Couch Potato...

I am here working hard on your orders.

Let me tell you about a few new things we have added to help speed up your order. First we are computerizing the way we process your order so that we can more easily look it up if we need to and maintain our customer list. The program will also help us process our shipping information by including weight, location and ordering information which will be essential if you have a question or complaint (Heavens Forbid).

We are now using UPS more than the post office. This helps in many ways including tracing a package if it is lost and in more speedily getting your package to you because they are quicker. . They are also more careful with shipments and they arrive in better condition. UPS costs a little more than post office, This is unfortunate but we feel you will find that it is worth it.

Also please note our new discount program. Discounts range from 5% to 20% off.

So things are looking up in 1988 for Coach Potato.

I really appreciate your orders and time but I really must get back to the tube...

The Phantom
The Green Hornet
The Shadow
The Batman

Each issue of Serials Adventures Presents offers 100 or more pages of pure nostalgic fun for $16.95

SERIALS ADVENTURES MAGAZINE

Flash Gordon Part One
Flash Gordon Part Two
Blackhawk

Each issue of Serials Adventures Presents features a chapter by chapter review of a rare serial combined with biographies of the stars and behind-the-scenes information. Plus rare photos. See the videotapes and read the books!

THE U.N.C.L.E. TECHNICAL MANUAL

Every technical device completely detailed and blueprinted, including weapons, communications, weaponry, organization, facitilites... 80 pages. 2 volumes...$9.95 each

NUMBER SIX: THE COMPLEAT PRISONER

The most unique and intelligent television series ever aired! Patrick McGoohan's tour-de-force of spies and mental mazes finally explained episode by episode, including an interview with the McGoohan and the complete layout of the real village!...160 pages...$14.95

THE GREEN HORNET

Daring action adventure with the Green Hornet and Kato. This show appeared before Bruce Lee had achieved popularity but delivered fun, superheroic action. Episode guide and character profiles combine to tell the whole story...120 pages...$14.95

WILD, WILD, WEST

Is it a Western or a Spy show? We couldn't decide so we're listing it twice. Fantastic adventure, convoluted plots, incredible devices...all set in the wild, wild west! Details of fantastic devices, character profiles and an episode-by-episode guide...120 pages...$17.95

THE FREDDY KRUEGER STORY

The making of the monster. Including interviews with director Wes Craven and star Robert Englund. Plus an interview with Freddy himself! $14.95

THE ALIENS STORY

Interviews with movie director James Cameron, stars Sigourney Weaver and Michael Biehn and effects people and designers Ron Cobb, Syd Mead, Doug Beswick and lots more!...$14.95

ROBOCOP

Law enforcement in the future. Includes interviews with the stars, the director, the writer, the special effects people, the storyboard artists and the makeup men! $16.95

MONSTERLAND'S HORROR IN THE '80s

The definitive book of the horror films of the '80s. Includes interviews with the stars and makers of Aliens, Freddy Krueger, Robocop, Predator, Fright Night, Terminator and all the others! $17.95

LOST IN SPACE

THE COMPLEAT LOST IN SPACE
244 PAGES...$17.95

TRIBUTE BOOK
Interviews with everyone!...$7.95

TECH MANUAL
Technical diagrams to all of the special ships and devices plus exclusive production artwork....$9.95

GERRY ANDERSON

SUPERMARIONATION
Episode guides and character profiles to Capt Scarlet, Stingray, Fireball, Thunderbirds, Supercar and more...240 pages...$17.95

BEAUTY AND THE BEAST

THE UNOFFICIAL BEAUTY & BEAST
Complete first season guide including interviews and biographies of the stars.
132 pages
$14.95

DARK SHADOWS

DARK SHADOWS TRIBUTE BOOK
Interviews, scripts and more...
160 pages...$14.95

DARK SHADOWS INTERVIEWS BOOK
A special book interviewing the entire cast.
$18.95

DOCTOR WHO THE BAKER YEARS

A complete guide to Tom Baker's seasons as the Doctor including an in-depth episode guide, interviews with the companions and profiles of the characters...
300 pages...$19.95

THE DOCTOR WHO ENCYCLOPEDIA: THE FOURTH DOCTOR

Encyclopedia of every character, villain and monster of the Baker Years.
..240 pages...$19.95

THE COUCH POTATO BOOK CATALOG 5715 N BALSAM, LAS VEGAS, NV 89130

THE ILLUSTRATED STEPHEN KING

A complee guide to the novels and short stories of Stephen King illustrated by Steve Bissette and others...$12.95

GUNSMOKE YEARS

The definitive book of America's most successful television series. 22 years of episode guide, character profiles, interviews and more...240 pages, $14.95

THE REST OF THE SHOW

THE KING COMIC HEROES

The complete story of the King Features heroes including Prince Valiant, Flash Gordon, Mandrake, The Phantom, Secret Agent, Rip Kirby, Buz Sawyer, Johnny Hazard and Jungle Jim. These fabulous heroes not only appeared in comic strips and comic books but also in movies and serials, Includes interviews with Hal Foster, Al Williamson and Lee Falk...$14.95

Special discounts are available for library, school, club or other bulk orders. Please inquire.

IF YOUR FAVORITE TELEVISION SERIES ISN'T HERE, LET US KNOW... AND THEN STAY TUNED!

And always remember that if every world leader was a couch potato and watched TV 25 hours a day, 8 days a week, there would be no war...

THE COUCH POTATO BOOK CATALOG 5715 N BALSAM, LAS VEGAS, NV 89130

Boring, but Necessary Ordering Information!

Payment: All orders must be prepaid by check or money order. Do not send cash. All payments must be made in US funds only.

Shipping: We offer several methods of shipment for our product.

Postage is as follows:

For books priced under $10.00— for the first book add $2.50. For each additional book under $10.00 add $1.00. (This is per individual book priced under $10.00, not the order total.)

For books priced over $10.00— for the first book add $3.25. For each additional book over $10.00 add $2.00. (This is per individual book priced over $10.00, not the order total.)

These orders are filled as quickly as possible. Sometimes a book can be delayed if we are temporarily out of stock. You should note on your order whether you prefer us to ship the book as soon as available or send you a merchandise credit good for other TV goodies or send you your money back immediately. Shipments normally take 2 or 3 weeks, but allow up to 12 weeks for delivery.

Special UPS 2 Day Blue Label RUSH SERVICE: Special service is available for desperate Couch Potatos. These books are shipped within 24 hours of when we receive your order and should take 2 days to get from us to you.

For the first **RUSH SERVICE** book under $10.00 add $4.00. For each additional 1 book under $10.00 and $1.25. (This is per individual book priced under $10.00, not the order total.)

For the first **RUSH SERVICE** book over $10.00 add $6.00. For each additional book over $10.00 add $3.50 per book. (This is per individual book priced over $10.00, not the order total.)

Canadian and Foreign shipping rates are the same except that Blue Label RUSH SERVICE is not available. All Canadian and Foreign orders are shipped as books or printed matter.

DISCOUNTS! DISCOUNTS! Because your orders are what keep us in business we offer a discount to people that buy a lot of our books as our way of saying thanks. On orders over $25.00 we give a 5% discount. On orders over $50.00 we give a 10% discount. On orders over $100.00 we give a 15% discount. On orders over $150.00 we give a 20% discount. Please list alternates when possible. Please state if you wish a refund or for us to backorder an item if it is not in stock.

100% satisfaction guaranteed. We value your support. You will receive a full refund as long as the copy of the book you are not happy with is received back by us in reasonable condition. No questions asked, except we would like to know how we failed you. Refunds and credits are given as soon as we receive back the item you do not want.

Please have mercy on Phyllis and carefully fill out this form in the neatest way you can. Remember, she has to read a lot of them every day and she wants to get it right and keep you happy! You may use a duplicate of this order blank as long as it is clear. **Please don't forget to include payment! And remember, we _love_ repeat friends...**

■■■■■■■■■■■■■■■■■■■■■■■■<u>ORDER FORM</u>■■■■■■■■■■■■■■■■■■■■■■■■■■■

_____The Phantom $16.95
_____The Green Hornet $16.95
_____The Shadow $16.95
_____Flash Gordon Part One $16.95_____Part Two $16.95
_____Blackhawk $16.95
_____Batman $16.95
_____The UNCLE Technical Manual One $9.95 _____Two $9.95
_____The Green Hornet Television Book $14.95
_____Number Six The Prisoner Book $14.95
_____The Wild Wild West $17.95
_____Trek Year One $10.95
_____Trek Year Two $12.95
_____Trek Year Three $12.95
_____The Animated Trek $14.95
_____The Movies $12.95
_____Next Generation $19.95
_____The Lost Years $14.95
_____The Trek Encyclopedia $19.95
_____Interviews Aboard The Enterprise $18.95
_____The Ultimate Trek $75.00
_____Trek Handbook $12.95_____Trek Universe $17.95
_____The Crew Book $17.95
_____The Making of the Next Generation $14.95
_____The Freddy Krueger Story $14.95
_____The Aliens Story $14.95
_____Robocop $16.95
_____Monsterland's Horror in the '80s $17.95
_____The Compleat Lost in Space $17.95
_____Lost in Space Tribute Book $9.95
_____Lost in Space Tech Manual $9.95
_____Supermarionation $17.95
_____The Unofficial Beauty and the Beast $14.95
_____Dark Shadows Tribute Book $14.95
_____Dark Shadows Interview Book $18.95
_____Doctor Who Baker Years $19.95
_____The Doctor Who Encyclopedia:The 4th Doctor $19.95
_____Illustrated Stephen King $12.95
_____Gunsmoke Years $14.95

```
┌─────────────────────────────────────────┐
│                                          │
│  NAME:_____  │
│                                          │
│  STREET:_____  │
│                                          │
│  CITY:_____  │
│                                          │
│  STATE:_____  │
│                                          │
│  ZIP:_____  │
│                                          │
│  TOTAL:_____  SHIPPING_____    │
│  SEND TO: COUCH POTATO,INC.              │
│      5715 N BALSAM, LAS VEGAS, NV  89130  │
└─────────────────────────────────────────┘
```